The Women Who Broke All the Rules

How the Choices of a Generation Changed Our Lives

The Women Who Broke All the Rules

How the Choices of a Generation
Changed Our Lives

Susan B. Evans, Ed.D.   Joan P. Avis, Ph.D.

Sourcebooks, Inc.
Naperville, IL

Published by Sourcebooks, Inc.
P.O. Box 4410
Naperville, IL 60567-4410
630.961.3900
Fax: 630.961.2168

Library of Congress Cataloging-in-Publication Data
Evans, Susan, Ed.D.
    The women who broke all the rules: how the choices of a generation changed
    our lives/Susan Evans and Joan Avis.
        p.   cm.
    ISBN 1-57071-430-4 (alk. paper).—ISBN 1-57071-428-2 (pbk.: alk. paper)
    1. Women—United States—Case studies. 2. Success—United States—Case
    studies. 3. Self-realization—United States—Case studies. 4. Baby boom genera-
    tion—United States. 5. Social change—United States. I. Avis, Joan. II. Title.
HQ 1421.E94 1998
305.42'0973—dc21   98-8498
                                                                       CIP

Printed and bound in the United States of America
VHG   10 9 8 7 6 5 4 3 2

"A generation must tacitly agree to remember certain things in certain ways and refuse to be dissuaded from its chosen version of the past. Otherwise the past won't stay put. If we're not vigilant about preserving our own history, someone will always come along and try to correct our memories. And how then will we know who we were or who we are now?"

—**Barbara Raskin, author**

Dedication

In honor of the memory of our dear friend,
Elizabeth Dean Bigelow, Ph.D.

(June 28, 1940–December 17, 1988)

TABLE OF CONTENTS

Acknowledgments

We want to thank many special people without whom this book would never have been written, beginning with our parents, Blanche and Maclyn Besserman and Mathilda and John Piekarski, who provided us with unconditional love and the encouragement to succeed at whatever we set out to do.

We deeply appreciate the wonderful women we interviewed for the book who openly and honestly shared their lives with us. They are outstanding representatives of the Torchbearer Generation and we hope we have done justice to their remarkable stories.

Those who never doubted we would complete this book and supported us over the years without question deserve special recognition: Tony Martinez, Jim Lewis, Lloyd Lewis, Martin Connelly, Daryl Nardick, Rachel Fitzgerald, and Ester Deel. Our pets, Guapa and Nelson, kept us company and gave us unwavering loyalty.

We especially want to pay tribute to our lifelong and more recent friends, too numerous to mention individually, who created the context in which we have been able to live such rich lives. We thank our colleagues at the University of San Francisco School of Education, particularly the Women's Faculty Group, for providing us with a real sense of community.

We also want to acknowledge the four significant environments where we lived while we wrote the book: San Francisco, CA; Berkeley, CA; San Miguel de Allende, Mexico; and Puerto Morelos, Mexico.

Several individuals merit thanks for providing assistance in book preparation: Beverly Cooke, Vicky Godinez, Mark Levine, Deborah Miller, Tamara Monosoff, and Cindy Paiva. We especially want to recognize Teresa Wilson, whose editorial feedback from the perspective of a woman from a different generation was invaluable. We thank our publisher Dominique Raccah for her faith in us and the book, along with editors Todd Stocke and Jennifer Fusco and the hardworking staff at Sourcebooks.

Finally, and most significantly, we thank each other. After five years of working on the book, our mutual respect, admiration, and friendship have only deepened and grown!

Preface

"I have often thought of myself and my friends as transitional figures, more sure of where we were coming from than where we were going. Friends of mine have described our coming of age as being on the cusp of changes that fundamentally redefined the role of women."

—Hillary Rodham Clinton

For six years, we have been exploring the lives of the generation of women who were in their teens and early twenties during the period of historically unprecedented social change that began in America in the late 1960s. As researchers and members of this generation ourselves, we became personally and professionally curious about leading-edge baby-boomer women who evolved the vast array of professional and personal choices which women of all ages now take for granted. With courage, resilience, and wisdom, they redefined adult womanhood and made significant achievements with few role models or mentors and little social support. How have they been able to accomplish this? What can we learn from their experiences that will enable others to lead healthier and more directed lives?

In an attempt to answer these questions, we began a large-scale descriptive research study of the generation of women, now in their forties to early fifties, who came of age at a certain point in American social history. We used both qualitative and quantitative research methods to accomplish three objectives: 1) to gauge the impact this generation has had on contemporary behaviors, practices, and standards; 2) to explore female adult development in terms of psychological well-being and life transitions; and 3) to identify functional personal and professional strategies which emanated from this generation as models for others. As social scientists and college professors, we have been teaching graduate students in education and psychology and conducting research for over twenty years. We each bring a unique perspective to this investigation. Susan has taught university courses in survey and descriptive research, data analysis, and women's studies. In her capacity as a counseling psychologist, Joan has worked with clients for twenty-five years; as a professor, she teaches in the areas of adult development and life transitions counseling. We are also close friends who have enjoyed lifelong, deep friendships with women who are members of this demographic group.

The criteria for selecting participants for this study were fairly specific. We wanted to identify women, born between 1945 and 1955, who had been continuously in the workforce since completing their education and who viewed their lives as containing both conventional and unconventional life choices

and experiences. Further, these women would perceive themselves, and be perceived by others, as professionally self-made
and psychologically healthy. We also wanted to identify a representative subset of women from a cross section of heterogeneous
geographic, professional, and personal backgrounds.

We found participants, and they found us, through a variety of ways. We attended many meetings of business and professional groups with large female memberships including events
held in grand ballrooms as well as informal potluck suppers in
private homes. At these gatherings, we distributed flyers
announcing our interest in finding potential subjects for this
research. We also asked associates and friends to refer women
from diverse backgrounds and locations. Finally, we placed ads
in professional newsletters, posted notices at health clubs, and
spoke to colleagues in a variety of academic settings about our
interest in meeting women who are members of this generation.

Using this snowball sampling technique, referrals came
quickly. There were self-referrals from women who had seen a
flyer or heard about our research from a co-worker or friend,
women who were recommended by a daughter or step-daughter
or an employee or colleague, as well as women who were known
to those already in the study. We made many phone calls and
spoke, sometimes at length, with potential interviewees. Only a
handful of women who were contacted declined to participate.
One hundred women of diverse cultural backgrounds who had
grown up in suburbs, in big cities, and on farms across thirty-four
states were interviewed for this book. Most come from middle-
class backgrounds and are college-educated. The final sample
includes a majority of Caucasian women as well as a smaller but

representative subset of Asian, Hispanic, and African-American women. Most are heterosexual, but gay and bisexual women also participated in the study.

We decided to use two- to three-hour face-to-face interviews as the primary method of data collection. In order to have a standardized set of questions, we designed an interview questionnaire specifically for this investigation. Our initial attempt at developing a questionnaire was informative but incomplete. The women who were in the pilot test group seemed to thoroughly enjoy themselves, but when we read transcripts of those interviews, we saw that there were serious gaps in the information we had set out to gather. Because our interests were two-fold—first, female adult development and the process by which lives unfold, and second, the impact of this generation—we saw that our purposes would be better served if we restructured the questionnaire into two sections.

The first section is a chronological life history survey, an autobiographical portrait of the interviewees from childhood to the present, focusing on three key elements: 1) the conventional and unconventional aspects at each stage of development; 2) the key turning points across the life span; and 3) the "unique" aspects and experiences during each era as elicited through personal anecdotes and specific probes. For each decade, we also asked, "If you were an author, how would you title this chapter of your life?" This section is followed by a series of self-reflective questions on a variety of issues which allow each woman to consider her own role, as well as the role of her generation, in forging new ways for adult women to live. These questions address why their lives have turned out as they have, whether they view themselves as pioneers, whether they identify themselves as feminists, their advice to younger women, their future plans, how they reconcile their 1950s childhoods with their more liberated adult selves, and their reflections on the role men, women, and families play in their lives. For sample description purposes, each interviewee completed a demographic data sheet that elicited information on: year and place of birth; work, marital, and educational history; number of children; spouse's, parents', and siblings' education and occupation; religious upbringing; and current income.

We spent one year traveling and conducting interviews with ordinary women who told us stories that were as extraordinary as they were universal. All were eager to talk about their lives and pleased to contribute to a greater understanding of stable, successful, and happy mid-life women. Interviews were conducted in offices, in hotel lobbies, on back porches, in kitchens and living rooms, and sometimes in the homes of out-of-town friends who provided a place to work.

We decided that in order to get the most out of each interview we would mail the questions one week to ten days in advance. This gave each woman the choice of preparing for the interview or not. Few chose the latter. In fact, most came prepared with pages and pages of recollections, both cherished and painful, and insights about what it meant to be part of a generation for whom the rules changed as they entered adolescence and young adulthood. As researchers, it was a great privilege to be a part of these interviews. We were awed by stories of incredible triumph and moved by accounts of betrayal and loss. What we did not anticipate was the wide variety of routes women this age have taken in their pursuit of autonomy and access to the mainstream.

While each interview was different, all were similar in three ways. First, we were surprised and grateful for the degree of honesty and openness with which each woman approached the interview. We were taken aback with their candor because we had not expected such a high level of trust on their part—we were, after all, strangers to each other. Second, it was clear that they loved being interviewed. Women who made it clear at the outset that they only had two hours were soon on the telephone canceling their next appointment in order to tell their story fully and not in haste. Third, because each interview included an across-the-lifespan review of pivotal events and significant turning points from childhood to the present, tears invariably were shed.

We heard over and over, "I wish this interview could go on for another three hours!" Clearly being able to share one's life story with an attentive listener is a too rare event in the lives of most people. Even those who know us best may be unaware of some of the most significant and formative events in our lives. For this reason, we have included the interview questionnaire in the Appendix of the book so that readers may interview themselves or their women friends.

Data collection, transcription, and data organization were enormous tasks. Each interview was tape recorded and typed for later analysis. We sent each interviewee a full copy of her own transcript for her review and for final approval to include the material in the book with identifier changes. After reading their transcripts, only two women declined to participate further.

Incorporating the stories into flowing narratives proved to be a challenging task since spoken language is very different from the written word. We hope that those whom we interviewed feel we have done justice to the meaning and spirit of their experiences if not their exact verbiage.

The transfer of audio taped interviews into typed transcripts was tedious and time-consuming but essential in order to content analyze the data. We initially read the transcripts to identify key themes which emerged from the material and to select stories that best exemplified those themes. The goal was to use their life stories to illustrate the vast social and cultural changes that the women of this generation have experienced and effected over the last thirty years. Our intention was to present more than a collection of interesting anecdotes about leading-edge baby-boomer women. Rather, we hoped to frame the experiences of a remarkable generation contextually around key thematic ideas which emerged from this study. When we conceived of the idea for this book, we had some initial hunches about fundamental elements and issues that might surface. In fact, many of these hunches were confirmed by the sheer number of times similar ideas were expressed. This suggests that there are common experiences which resonate for women of this generation. Because the data were analyzed nomothetically (across subjects) as well as idiographically (individually), we were able to identify and examine patterns across all one hundred subjects.

Based on this analysis, the results of this research are presented in two sections. The first part of the book is organized chronologically and developmentally to cover the first four decades of their lives from the 1950s to the present. In these chapters, the focus is on significant turning points and cross-roads including breaking away and individuating from families, entering new professional arenas, and recovering from detours and roadblocks such as failed marriages or self-destructive behaviors. The second part of the book addresses the larger generational issues which cut across the experiences of all those we interviewed, including their relationships with others in their lives and the lifestyle choices that clearly differentiate them from their mother's generation. Throughout the book, we use the concept of "Old Rule" and "New Truth" to differentiate between the precepts under which this generation was raised and the principles that they forged as a generation.

This book is not about well-known public figures. Rather it is about typical women who represent a very untypical generation. We have been inspired, shocked, amused, and amazed by their stories and we are certain you will be too. By sharing their lives with you, we hope to honor this generation for their ability to profit from their experiences, prevail over daunting life events, and build satisfying, productive lives. As a generation, they took advantage of emerging opportunities to create new social standards and became prototypes for personal growth in adulthood. They are, in every way, self-made women who until now have received little credit for literally reinventing female adulthood. This book is a tribute to the women who broke all the rules and whose choices changed our lives.

The Women Who Broke All the Rules

How the Choices of a Generation

Changed Our Lives

Part One

Who We Are As Women

Chapter One

I See Myself as an Accidental Pioneer

"If you could talk to the women who came across America in covered wagons, they'd say they weren't very tough either. I did what I had to do. That was the case for most of my generation. It was all timing. We never set out to blaze trails, yet in so many ways, we did."

The generation born between 1945 and 1955, the first decade of the baby boom, is the first in which vast numbers of American women chose to deviate from conventional patterns of education, marriage, childbearing, and careers. Raised with the traditional female expectations of the 1950s—to go to college, get married, and have a family—they encountered unanticipated events in adolescence and early adulthood which changed the course of their lives. Like Sleeping Beauty, an entire generation was awakened by the collective energy of the radical counterculture, the civil-rights movement, and second-wave feminism. Because these women entered young adulthood in the late 1960s, a time of enormous social change, their thoughts and actions directly challenged society's narrow and stifling rules for girls. They became accidental pioneers in the process, going where women had never gone before.

Remarkably, this generation went beyond conventional limits and rules in their twenties, thirties, and forties, not just during adolescence. As teenagers and young adults, they began the lifelong process of being risk-takers, bold in their pursuit of both professional and personal success. When the doors to traditionally male professions swung open, they were among the first women to take advantage of emerging opportunities. When they weren't challenging the assumptions about who could enter certain occupations, they were breaking every rule in the "good girl" handbook. They defied the sanctions against interracial and interfaith marriage, abortion, single motherhood, divorce, and unmarried cohabitation which, at one time, were big violations of social mores for middle-class females. They led the way by showing that women could engage in such conduct and still be respectable people, by any standards.

The story of this transitional generation is a contemporary version of the classic pioneer tale of self-transformation and triumph over adversity. Like early pioneers, these women took different roads, made distinctly different choices than their predecessors, and learned that those who "go first" face difficult times when they reject established social and cultural conventions. Unlike early pioneer women who left home with their husbands and families, these women had only each other to buffer what they encountered along the way and their journey still continues to have profound and far-reaching implications for how society views women. Despite relentless efforts over the last thirty years to rein them back in, this generation boldly refused to accept second-class status on the basis of their sex and created unprecedented life options for all women, not just for themselves. Because we see their lives as prototypes for all women learning how to survive and thrive, we call the women of this generation Torchbearers. Torchbearers initiate, originate, break new ground, and scout unknown trails. As transmitters of the light of knowledge, they also have the responsibility to pass the torch to those who follow.

The women of this generation were forced, out of necessity, to meet the challenge of integrating valuable lessons from the past with abundant new ways of being. Through the course of their adult development, they pioneered previously unheard of freedoms and choices for women that most now take for granted and constructed empowered lives by devising new ways to love and work. As a result of their efforts, women today are truly free to become fully self-actualized persons, without the constraints of gender. We want to honor this amazing and resourceful generation for their sense of spirit and adventure, their ability to triumph over obstacles, and their creativity in crafting an entirely new model for female adult development. Theirs is a living legacy that must be shared with women of all ages.

The bold statements we just made about the generation of women who broke all the rules may seem obvious to some, but if they are so obvious, why haven't we read about their incredible, inspirational lives in the media and popular press? In fact, the opposite is the case. With the exception of some feminist writers, few have publicly extolled the virtues of this generation.

Apart from articles about famous members, such as Oprah Winfrey, Hillary Rodham Clinton, Diane Keaton, and Amy Tan, we found very little in the popular literature that commends this generation as special and unique. Instead, they have been characterized as selfish, anti-male, unappealing and unattractive, neurotic, narcissistic, and anti-life, to name just a few. While we knew intuitively from our personal experience that this picture was distorted, it wasn't until after we finished our interviews with one hundred ordinary but extraordinary representatives of this generation that even we fully realized the extent and depth of their impact on womankind.

Where Are the Men?

Six years ago, an event took place which initially brought the contributions of this remarkable generation to our attention. Susan went to a friend's "ladies only" birthday party. A dozen women, all in their late thirties to forties, had been invited. Although most were strangers, among women this is never a barrier to lively conversation and instant self-revelation. Halfway through the evening, Susan turned to a friend and said, "There are twelve smart, interesting, attractive women here—how come everyone is single?" That was the first of many questions to follow.

When Susan met Joan for lunch the next day, this observation from the previous evening became Topic A. Like most women, we had read the flawed, yet highly publicized, Yale study about the man shortage for women over age thirty-five. Were these dozen vital, financially secure, successful women living proof of the lack of available men or was their (non)marital status merely one element of a far more significant phenomenon? Being social scientists and in that age group ourselves, we decided to explore the issue further.

We began by examining the few facts we had about the women at the dinner party. First, they were all leading-edge baby boomers. Born in the decade after World War II, they came of age during the social, political, and cultural tumult that occurred in America in the late 1960s. Although much of society was playing by the old rules, young adolescent women recognized the real revolution that was taking place. Women's lives were about to be transformed forever and they would be both the agents and beneficiaries of that change. What was the process that transformed these young women into healthy, resilient adults?

Second, while these women had been continuously in the workforce since completing their education, not one was working in her original career. The social worker was now a computer executive. The art teacher was in marketing. The dancer ran an executive search company. And so on. All had chosen different careers after trying more traditional female options and discovering they could hold their own in "male" occupations. The broad framework of adult development emphasizes that growth occurs across the life span. What could be learned from women whose lives present models of continuous growth and change throughout adulthood?

Third, the lives of these women contained both highly conventional and highly unconventional experiences. As a generation, they encountered the discrepancy between the traditional choices of their mothers and the nontraditional choices of their peers at every social, political, and cultural turn. Because they had few role models, women had to look to their own experiences and feelings to determine what was right, what was possible, and what to do next. In the process, they became a generation of adventurers, experimenters, explorers, and leaders. Like modern day wagon-train pioneers, they led the way into the uncharted territory between the narrowly defined landscape of the 1950s and the unexplored radical terrain of the 1970s. How had they reconciled and integrated the incongruous messages from these two eras?

Several months later, we happened to talk informally with some women who had been at the birthday party. We confirmed that they were professionally self-made and psychologically healthy. Not surprisingly, most had been married or had lived with a partner at least once. More significantly, we discovered that the majority were involved in happy, loving relationships. One forty-one-year-old was engaged and about to marry for the first time. Another had a long-term monogamous yet non-cohabiting relationship. Still another was about to move to Europe with her partner.

By now, our curiosity had moved beyond the original question that sparked our interest and the experiences of a dozen women to a much bigger picture—the picture of an entire generation. We wondered how the women in this age group had emerged from a confusing and conflicted historical period into healthy and fulfilled adults, how they created meaningful lives they never envisioned as children, and how they transformed their old ways of thinking about themselves as women. Our personal experiences and conversations with friends informed our thinking about what directions we might take to find answers.

Many lunches and discussions later, we decided to apply our professional expertise and skills to the topic. Soon we had developed a set of questions that would enable us to gain insights into two key areas: women's adult development and the impact of a unique generation. After a year of identifying and interviewing women, most of whom we had never met before, we began to analyze and synthesize their individual stories and to identify the old rules and new truths which captured the continuity of their learning from childhood to the present. In the process, we gained a broader perspective on their significance as a generation.

We suspect that every woman of this generation has a story to tell—an untold story in most cases—that chronicles her choices, her hopes and dreams, her fears, and her efforts to do her best and evolve new truths from old, outdated rules. That is, of course, the point. This book provides a vehicle for many of these stories to be heard. By including our interview questions in the Appendix, we invite you to tell your life story and to listen to the reflections of your friends. But more importantly, our purpose is to frame these individual stories in the context of female adult development which results from having lived during a unique historical period. Our hope is that you will gain new appreciation of your own life choices and feel increased pride for your place in the generation of women who broke all the rules.

Do Women Grow and Change In Adulthood?

Daniel Levinson's *Seasons of a Man's Life* and Gail Sheehy's *Passages* brought to mainstream America a new idea—that development doesn't stop after childhood ends but, in fact, continues across the lifespan. They proposed that adults had defined "tasks" to accomplish for each stage and decade, with revisions of one's life course resulting from age-defined periods of re-examination. Other views of growth, such as William Bridges' Transitions, suggest that more fluid, complex patterns of development based on life events and self-initiated transitions are the major sources of change in adulthood. In reflecting on this generation, we hypothesized that their development was shaped not only by their chronological age and life transitions, but also by the unique historical circumstances they encountered along the way.

From our examination of their lives, we concluded that these women not only contributed to challenging the old rules about adulthood, but significantly advanced the shift in our collective thinking about development over the past few decades. The old static definition of adulthood as a time of limited change and consolidation has been replaced with a new realization that life presents an extended opportunity for learning. The growing interest in healthy aging, wellness, psychological well-being, and positive mental health all point to this new view. Researchers Carol Ryff and Corey Lee Keyes, in a 1995 *Journal of Personality and Social Psychology* article, identified six dimensions of well-being in adults: self acceptance, positive relations with others, autonomy, environmental mastery, purpose in life, and personal growth. Not coincidentally, we discovered that the women we interviewed possess all of these characteristics. Why have we read or heard so little about their positive attributes?

Popular literature and the media have devoted little attention to the strengths of this generation of women. Instead, we found countless self-help books that claim many successful women have "female problems," including burnout, infertility, spinsterhood, and codependency. This finger-pointing at the lifestyle choices made by contemporary women presents an erroneous image of this generation and undermines their hard-won gains in both professional and personal arenas. Because of what we learned about the resilience, resourcefulness, and life satisfaction of the women we interviewed, we felt compelled to document, illustrate, and celebrate this generation's positive contributions to defining healthy female development.

The Generation of Women Who Broke All the Rules

In order to function effectively in a changing world, the women born between 1945 and 1955 had to let go of almost all their childhood expectations and create a new reality. In the course of meeting the challenge to construct meaningful lives, as a generation, they evolved new principles for living to replace the old rules. They used creativity, courage, and determination to redefine womanhood in the process. In fact, their hard work has become so much a part of every woman's experience today that it is too easy to forget that there was a time when most women valued conformity, were afraid to take risks, and lacked self-confidence.

Born into a time when assimilating new experiences into old structures no longer worked, these women were forced to construct new frameworks for thinking about themselves as adults. Along the way, they gained inner strength and an ability to problem solve in a wide variety of situations. We believe that every woman who remembers when her future was defined by limited opportunity and inferior status has spent the last thirty years on a personal mission to redefine and transform female adulthood.

Moving back and forth from disequilibrium to balance, the lives of Torchbearers revealed insights women of all ages can use to lead productive, satisfying lives. By gathering their stories, we came to see how these women gained increased self-confidence and an ability to continually redefine themselves as they encountered new and sometimes daunting situations. Through reflecting on their stories, we affirmed our expectation that ordinary women can be quite extraordinary in the ways they create meaning in their lives. From analyzing their stories, we confirmed that female adult development is not just about who we are inside, but also about the influence of historical and cultural events on the collective experience of women.

We discovered that women of this generation are persistent workers and risk-takers who recognized opportunities and took advantage of them. Women, in general, have great difficulty taking credit for their success. Cutting-edge baby boomers who walk the tightrope every day between the worlds of femininity and feminism are particularly prone to self-effacing statements, even when all evidence points to the contrary. Men have less trouble taking credit for their achievements. This book was written to encourage Torchbearers to take pride in their incredible accomplishments and contributions to healthy living for women of all ages.

Our decision to focus the book on this generation as viewed through a developmental lens has been both rewarding and educational. We traced the process by which new principles for living evolved from their young adulthood to the present in order to capture the on-going nature of their learning. We found that contemporary women could incorporate very different aspects of themselves into functional personal identities, including roles and attributes traditionally associated with being male in our society. Women of this generation have expanded the world of possibilities not only for themselves, but for all women. We hope we have done justice to the diverse individual approaches they used to effect change in themselves and in society and that we have provided a fresh perspective on their immense contributions which have yet to be fully acknowledged and appreciated. Finally, we encourage all women to see themselves in the stories we chronicle, to gather in informal groups of friends to share their own stories with each other, and to never forget those who helped them become more than they ever thought they could be.

Chapter Two

By the Time I Got to College,
They Changed All the Rules

"When Everygirl was a little girl she learned a valuable lesson: she couldn't get what she wanted by asking for it. Being a good Everygirl meant shutting up and pleasing others."

—Cynthia Heimel, author

More than eighteen million women were born between 1945 and 1955. Raised in the traditional ways of the 1950s, they were programmed to follow a lockstep sequence from school to marriage to motherhood. Like their mothers and older sisters, they were expected to devote their adult lives to husband, home, and family. Instead, at a time when they were just old enough to act independently but still young enough not to have made any irrevocable life choices, America was swept up in a youth frenzy. In 1966, *Time* selected as its Man of the Year "the men and women twenty-five and under." The magazine explained its choice this way, "Never have the young been so assertive or so articulate." The Youth Culture was born and suddenly the whole world wanted to be young or, barring that, act young. Cheryl Merser, author of *Grown-ups*, writes, "Our generation had mastered youth in a way no other generation in history ever had. Where earlier generations rushed their youths along, we wanted to stretch ours out. Moreover, we were envied by many in the older generation—we weren't imitating them, they were imitating us."

When the momentum of the civil rights and feminist movements extended personal and professional opportunities for women and minorities, millions of young women set out to become everything their mothers could not. Although few joined an organized movement to change the world, by virtue of their date of birth they became part of the *Zeitgeist*, the spirit of the times. By coming of age when dramatic changes were occurring in women's options and life patterns, women were both susceptible to and responsible for molding the forces that also were shaping their futures. In the process, the women of this generation had to create their own norms. Males their age had older successful men to emulate; women did not. Beginning their young adulthoods ill-prepared to take on the world, they did exactly that, and by deviating from past patterns of love and work, created adult lifestyles they had never dreamed of as children.

Father Knows Best?

As children, millions of us were mesmerized by the television program *Father Knows Best*, an idealized vision of the American suburban family. The Andersons, Jim, Margaret, Bud, Kathy, and

Princess, were a Norman Rockwell illustration come to life. But behind that "mom and apple pie" picture was another impression of the 1950s as fear-driven, rule-bound, and conformist.

Most young girls saw the discrepancy between their own families, whose problems could not be solved in thirty minutes, and the perfect Andersons. At home, the rule that "father knows best" often translated into authoritarian, tyrannical parenting, with mother denying conflict and smoothing things over. The predominant message communicated to little girls was that the extended world was not to be experienced, but feared. While television shows and models of womanhood were designed to emphasize the value of staying close to home, strong societal and parental controls left many young girls feeling trapped. Torchbearers remember the contradictions of this era: the image of the happy nuclear family juxtaposed with frantic efforts to keep everybody in line.

Much of what was done or said in the 1950s was governed by inhibition and prohibition, particularly for females. Tremendous importance was placed on keeping up appearances as well as behaving modestly, courteously, and most of all conventionally. Girls were brought up to center their attention on others rather than themselves, to set aside their own aspirations and interests, and as author Catherine Bateson writes, "to bend to exterior winds." Most young girls understood the rules which governed their behavior, even if these rules were unspoken.

Emily Hancock, author of *The Girl Within*, describes how a young girl's personhood could be subdued, "Well before puberty, along comes the culture with the pruning shears, ruthlessly trimming back her spirit. Elders deflate her 'grandiose' ideas, labeling her strengths and interests unfeminine. She is expected to conform, to 'behave like a young lady.' She is defined as female instead of as a person. She gives up 'doing' in favor of 'being' a good girl; instead of suiting herself, she tries to please those around her. Impressed with the importance of others' opinions, she molds herself to what she thinks they want her to be."

Many young girls, even those with happy childhoods began to look for a means to escape from family and social control. In this instance, the willingness to break from the past represents not only a separation from familiar customs and traditions, but also from a predetermined future. Historically, women have looked to others for protection, security, and direction. Yet, they eagerly broke away, en masse, from the culture of submission and obedience which had governed their mothers' and older sisters' lives. Perhaps most remarkable is how young these women were when they took these first tentative steps. What enabled them to conquer their fears and what new guidelines did they as a generation create to stand together in facing the world? In order to understand how these principles evolved, we examined the lives of women who first had to separate from the past in order to construct healthy new models for adult living.

Old Rule: There is only one right way to live.

> "You woke up one morning and there weren't any rules. You could do anything, which was astounding, frightening, exhilarating, and very confusing."

Sharon's life has turned out differently from the way she thought it would. "When I was in high school," she says, "I assumed I would go to college, get married, and have kids. I was a cheer-leader, so I thought I would be a coach's wife. I certainly didn't see myself as a forty-six-year-old single career woman living in Manhattan."

Sharon grew up in a lower middle-class family in a small industrial city in the Midwest. She is proud to say that she is an adult child of normal parents. "The most unconventional thing about my childhood is that I didn't come from a dysfunctional family. My parents showed me love that was as close to uncon-ditional as you could get." Yet, from the moment she left home for college in 1967, Sharon broke every rule in the good girls' handbook. The state university was ninety miles away, but for Sharon, those ninety miles might well have been nine hundred. The college newspaper, along with the theater and political sci-ence departments, were the pockets of radicalism. As the editor of the newspaper during the Kent State-Cambodia invasion years, Sharon spoke at rallies, participated in campus protests, and wrote fiery editorials protesting university and governmen-tal policies.

"My mother had me at nineteen and my nineteenth year was the age I changed the most. Everything I had been taught as a child was wiped out within a matter of months. In high school, I was sickeningly perfect. I wrote a fairly conservative essay for the high school newspaper criticizing Vietnam War protesters. Within months, I was on the other side of the issue. Eventually, you get to a place where you rebel against whatever it was you were brought up with. If you were raised by radical hippies in the Haight Ashbury, then you become a Young Republican. You find some way to stick it to your parents. During college, my parents and I never got along and it was all about politics. We were a national cliché."

Sharon changed quickly during the pivotal years, 1967 to 1971, when she went away to college. "I made a lot of mistakes and got heavily into drinking," she recalls. "In college, I lived in the dorm with a Fundamentalist Christian Bible Belt girl which really must have tested her faith. She prayed for me because I was drinking, coming in late, letting my grades go to hell, and getting into bad relationships. I screwed up so much, but I never got pregnant, arrested, or kicked out of school. While it looks like I did a complete turnaround and became this radical, AWOL person, I managed to graduate and fulfill my parents' dreams. I have a habit of pushing the envelope, but always recognizing the envelope is gigantic. No matter how far out I go, I can always come back."

Women like Sharon grew up with few female role models. Those they had, like Beryl Markham or Margaret Mead, were so exceptional they didn't seem real. Torchbearers developed their own strategies as they went along, enabling them to reset the bar and make their choices the norm. Sharon says, "Younger generations of women have something we never had. Us! There's not a right way to live anymore. My generation wanted freedom. The universe answered, 'You want freedom? Here, you've got it!' It was like being thrown into a pool and told to swim, never having had a lesson. All things considered, we've made it quite well. Most of us are still standing, relatively well adjusted, and happy. It was a trial by fire, but we made it in better shape than not, and that has given us an almost instant confidence that men have simply by existing."

New Truth: There are many ways to live. Find one
that is right for you.

What is most striking about the young women who grew up in
the 1950s is not how intent they were to escape from the narrow
and confining rule-bound world of their mothers, but how up-
beat and enthusiastic they were about leaving everything behind
despite the uncertainty this venture held. The primary vehicle
women like Sharon used to leave home was fairly standard:
going away to college. While her parents encouraged Sharon to
get her degree, they also expected that their daughter would
graduate, come home to settle down, marry, and have children.
Few people anticipated that the social upheaval of that era would
provide the opportunity for vast numbers of young women to
break from their families in a variety of unimaginable ways.

On the brink of young adulthood, they discovered a fresh
world filled with new choices, possibilities, adventures, and
temptations—and the last place they intended to go was back
home. Parents had difficulty accepting that their daughters had
changed radically from the obedient girls they had once known;
they were left with no choice but to let go of their conventional
aspirations as well as their once conventional daughters.

Sherry Ruth Anderson and Patricia Hopkins, co-authors of
Feminine Face of God, describe the process of breaking away,
"Every woman…at least once in her life, reaches the threshold
where the old concepts, ideals, and emotional meanings no
longer fit and each one chose to cross that threshold. Modern
women need to leave home—for independence, for breaking
through or breaking away from social roles, for learning how to

trust ourselves." Caught up in the sexual and political freedom of the era, nice girls used campus protests, communal living, religious cults, and a variety of other means to separate from their rule-bound pasts. Leaving home can represent a physical and psychological break from the past. Some returned home, but their years of rebellion and adventure enabled them to individuate from their families, even deeply beloved ones such as Sharon's.

Old Rule: You must conform in order to get approval.

"In the 1950s through a good part of the 1960s, there were lots of rules for girls and few choices. Then, overnight, the situation flipped 180 degrees and there were few rules and lots of choices. The force of that flip completely disrupted any thought I had of being in that old world. It was so compelling that I had to be pulled in. My perspective changed as did the course of my life. Every woman my age was affected in one form or another."

Anna always felt like an outsider, a nonconformist. She began rebelling in early childhood, a practice she continued into her early thirties when she divorced her abusive, Fundamentalist husband and struck out on her own. Her path to independence was not marked by a single event, but rather was shaped by one lifelong question: "If God is present, why can't I feel him?" Anna describes her family as provincial and straight. And herself? "I was always rebellious, free thinking, and high-spirited, but if I let that flow, I would get punished," she says. "I couldn't figure out why. I thought, 'What am I doing wrong?' I needed to subdue my real personality in order to earn my parents' approval."

When she was a young teen, Anna became fascinated by the study of religion and spirituality. Always looking for answers the church didn't provide, Anna often read books on philosophy and theology. In college, she turned to drugs and then to a religious sect in her "search for the spirit." After a nearly fatal incident when she was doing hallucinogens, Anna realized she was in too deep. Shortly thereafter, she became a born-again Christian. "I had the whole dichotomous experience of the '60s—the drugs, the free sex, and the radical political demonstrations from eighteen to twenty. Then I did a complete about-face with the Jesus movement for the next twelve years.

"A minister at a local underground church explained that through a Christ-centered existence, the Holy Spirit comes into your life and allows you to have a personal relationship with God. That was what I'd been looking for. I thought, 'If it doesn't work, it doesn't work, but I'm going to go for it and see what happens.' The Spirit did come into my life at that time, enabling me to make the break from drugs. My parents were totally freaked out when I told them I was born again. They wanted to put me into a mental hospital and have me watched! Eventually, my mother convinced my father that I was in better shape than she'd ever seen me and that he ought to leave me alone. I graduated from college, but I didn't seem to have a really clear direction except one—service to God."

Anna met her husband in 1977. They shared the same walk of faith and spiritual life. The marriage lasted six and a half years with a lot of hardship. Financial hardship. Sexual hardship. In-law hardship. They had no children—which was probably a blessing, according to Anna. It was a difficult marriage in which their expected husband and wife roles were "mish-mashed into faith." She even hesitated to tell her family or friends that her husband behaved violently because they had a "Godly marriage" and she felt ashamed. Anna recalls, "I instigated the divorce. It was a stand for myself and my 'self' responded! When I separated from my husband, I was thirty-two and I didn't know how I was going to make a living in the real world. After years of serving my marriage, my husband, and God, I was out of touch with what I wanted as an individual. I made a list of goals that had to be resolved: find a job, buy a house, replace my car, take a vacation I can afford...things I'd never done. At the top of the list was 'Know thyself.' That is always at the top of the list. Within five years, I managed to meet every goal except 'know thyself.' I will always be working in that direction."

New Truth: You can't lead your life for external approval. Seek your own blessings.

For young women entering adulthood in the late 1960s through the mid-1970s, a single dominant pattern of adult female development no longer existed. Even when they followed the script of "go to college and then get married" as Anna did, new twists and turns made these choices more complicated. Looking for personal meaning and a sense of belonging, Anna's quest for spiritual knowledge took her down two paths—drugs and religion—courses followed by others seeking identity and connection to a higher power. Anna says, "Because I had no role models, I would dive into the abyss and hope I'd fly." When her path turned into a dead end, she seized control of her life in both enterprising and clear-headed ways.

24

Both Anna's and Sharon's stories illustrate the role of personality and continuity in adult development. Anna's spiritual bent and Sharon's journalistic abilities were clearly present in their adolescent years. In spite of the unique situational events they experienced, their natural propensities significantly shaped and directed the course of their lives, including the breakaway years. While neither woman fully acknowledges the inner imperative she drew upon to survive the psychological upheaval of having dramatically broken so many childhood mandates, each uses similar metaphors—being thrown into a pool or diving into an abyss—to describe her own leap of faith.

Anna took a stand for her "self" in response to her own experiences. She found that no one can tell you that you have freedom if you don't believe it. "Freedom of choice is something you have to know from within," Anna says. "I was fooled by the appearance of things. I listened to other people's opinions. I wanted their approval and acceptance. Every woman needs to know she can take a stand for herself without external reference to the prevailing cultural standard, but it takes courage to configure your life to look the way you want—big courage."

Old Rule: You owe it to your parents to lead a normal life.

"In my mother's day, if you got married, raised a family, and your husband had a good job, society patted you on the back because you were doing the right thing. For women of my generation, there are so many more options that you have to constantly remind yourself that you're doing OK. You don't get that ready-made, pre-packaged acceptance.

There is no 'new tradition' that says you're going by the book. Women have to search to get that kind of affirmation."

June always had a complicated relationship with her mother, a woman she describes as both strong-willed and clutchy. June was so compliant that even her first rebellion was a small one—in her freshman year in college, she pierced her ears, something her mother had forbidden her to do. Yet, despite her overprotectiveness, June's mother was no dowdy, acquiescent housewife. She often wrote and produced shows for the local community theater group. June was sent to an excellent dance school in Dallas and often entertained in theatrical productions and recitals. However, when June considered the possibility of pursuing a professional career in dance, her parents rejected the notion. Her father said, "A nice Jewish girl isn't a dancer. Period." June enrolled at college where she received a degree in math with the intention of becoming a high school math teacher.

Because of newly drafted Equal Employment standards, there were opportunities in the business world for women with degrees in math. Upon graduation from college in the early 1970s, June was immediately offered a job with a bank. Working as a programmer, she continued taking dance classes at night. After four boring years, fed up with both the corporate environment and a relationship that wasn't going anywhere, June decided to quit her job to pursue dancing.

"After several months of auditions, I got a job as a showgirl in Las Vegas. I'd always dreamed of being a professional dancer. I made the same money dancing that I made at the bank. I thought, 'Who could complain?' My father flipped out. He said,

'You owe it to me to lead a normal life!' My mother tried to be positive. She said, 'It's not exactly what I envision for my daughter, but if you're excited, I'm excited.'

"I never danced topless, but I did have some great costumes. There was one G-string costume with a little bra top, a little jacket, little leggings, and little feather things. That was the most risqué outfit but I wore tights, so it wasn't like my parts were sticking out. That job lasted a year. I tried to break into television dancing, but I wasn't tall, thin, really long-legged, and blonde, so even though I was a good dancer, I didn't get those jobs. I danced and took odd jobs, mostly waitressing, but after two years, my dance career wasn't going anywhere. By then, dance was out of my system. At twenty-eight, I decided to take a job in the computer industry."

New Truth: You owe it to yourself to live an exceptional life.

Mothers of this era wanted their daughters to be stronger and better educated than they were, but the likelihood that someday their daughters would pursue nontraditional careers, live and travel alone, or raise families, with or without partners, simply wasn't a realistic concern. Many of the women we interviewed told us about their bright, and sometimes resentful mothers who urged them to become self-reliant yet, at the same time, to seek security and protection. Boomers were subject to two discrepant views: one from their mothers' generation for whom notions of decorum, obligation, and sacrifice were strong, and one from their peers who placed a high value on individual gratification and the belief that they were equal to men.

One Torchbearer, who owns a marketing research firm and lives with her boyfriend and his children, recalls the mixed message she heard from her mother. "All my life, my mother urged me to want to be different. 'Don't be like everybody else. Stand out from the crowd.' Then in the next breath she would tell me, 'Get married to a nice man with a good profession. Work for a while, but then give it up. You'll have children, a wonderful house, and a wonderful life.' So I was going to have an exciting life where I was going to be different from everybody else, but at the same time I was going to be a wife and mother. That was the paradox."

While her mother supported June's decision to dance, perhaps as a way of living out her own unfulfilled fantasies, June actually got to pursue her dream as a vocation, something her mother could only do as a hobby. It has taken June and her mother many years to reconcile each's aspirations with her own. Today, June is a successful business owner, a part-time aerobics instructor, a newlywed, and, at forty-two, a first-time mom. When we asked June why her life has turned out as it has, she said without hesitation, "My mother."

Old Rule: Always put other people's needs and expectations first.

"One thing that I liked about the '60s was that there were no judgment calls. I'd grown up on judgment calls for everything, so I had to establish my own code of ethics. No one was telling me what my limits were so I had to set a program for myself. Once I became independent, I started to make decisions from the inside rather than the outside."

For the first thirty years of her life, Sydney lived to please others—first her family and then her husband. On the surface, it appeared that Sydney was doing the normal things middle-class young women did. In terms of external structure, her life was very traditional, but with regard to the interior, she felt like she was walking on a tight rope. "Even as a little girl," she recalls, "something felt very wrong. I assumed it was me. My way of hiding my fears was to play the good person role, which I did for many years. When I looked at my parents, all I could see was how I was going to lead my life and I didn't like what I was looking at. I thought, 'I'm going to get married, I'm going to have two and a half kids, and I'm going to be miserable.' I was terrified because I knew I was going to marry this guy even though I didn't want to. I felt like I didn't have control." The external world had programmed her for a marriage that she knew wasn't going to be a happy one.

Sydney's sense of "no way out" became clear in college. "I was at a party and one of my professors cornered me and critically said, 'You don't know how to let go. You don't know how to live. You hold yourself back. Look at what you're missing!' I was so angry with him. No one had ever said that to me, but he was right. I was so stuck that I couldn't break out of it. I got married right after graduation. The night before the wedding my father pulled me aside and said, 'You don't have to go through with this if you don't want to.' We were having a big wedding with almost three hundred guests. I looked him straight in the eye and I lied. I said, 'Dad, don't be silly, I love him.' "

After she had been married a year, she received a hysterical phone call from her aunt who had just spoken to her run-away daughter, Sydney's cousin. No one had heard from this young woman in over four years. Literally delirious because of this news, Sydney went to pick up her husband at work. She walked into his office, told him the story, and exclaimed that she was prepared to fly to see her cousin the next day. Her husband told her, "You can't do that." She remembers that something inside of her actually clicked off at that moment. She couldn't talk to or look at her husband for three days. "I knew then that one day I would have the 'umphh' to leave him. The whole family accepted my cousin back with open arms, which gave me tremendous hope, because I had never rebelled. I knew that if I finally broke out of this horrible jail I felt I was in, things would be all right because they allowed her to come back into the family.

"In my second year of graduate school, I was still living with my husband. I went to a convention, met somebody, and fell deeply in love. I thought, 'My God, I'm married!' I was so prim and proper, I couldn't believe this was happening. I knew that this was the man I wanted to live my life with. I went to tell my parents that I was unhappy and wanted a divorce, which was an enormous, tremendous step for me. I was twenty-five, and this was the first time I had ever done anything to defy convention. My father said, 'You married him. You knew who he was. You loved him at the time. You make it work.' I was devastated but I didn't leave my husband."

The next year, Sydney's father got very sick. It was at this time Sydney and her siblings discovered that their father had cancer and had been in chemotherapy for two years. Twelve days later, he died. "After that, I divorced my husband," Sydney says. "In some ways, I finally became somewhat free. The other man didn't wait. He ended the relationship because he never thought I was going to get divorced. I finished graduate school and, at thirty-one, moved to the West Coast, which was something I'd always wanted to do. I didn't know anyone. I didn't have a plan in terms of money or a profession. But I had always had a dream that I was going to pick up and relocate where I didn't know anyone so I could make it on my own, whatever 'making it' meant. Financially, socially, or professionally, I didn't care. I wanted to live out my dream and know that I could *make it on my own*."

New Truth: Learn what your own needs are and honor them.

For many years, Sydney's life was affected by her guilt and conflict over a sense of obligation to her family and her own notions of self-fulfillment. Even as a married graduate student in her mid-twenties, she had not yet learned to rely on her own authority. Because she was trying so hard to be a good person and do all the "right" things, she was completely lost regarding her own needs, hopes, and dreams. She responded to other people's expectations about how they wanted her to lead her life, rather than listening to her own voice. She says, "I didn't know how to listen. There was too much that interfered with hearing myself." The death of her father finally enabled her to begin the process of cutting the cord that kept her tied to her controlling family and husband.

Recently, Sydney spoke to her cousin who had run away from home so many years before. Sydney asked her, "Why did you leave?" Her cousin said, "I didn't know who I was. Things were so confined and controlled." Her cousin's answer gave Sydney validation for how she had felt all those years. For the first time in her life, she felt whole. She says, "I no longer have a false self and a real self anymore—I've become integrated."

Old Rule: Your families' values, beliefs, and practices should be yours.

> *"I wanted to fly. When I was in high school, we had to write a paper about what we wanted to be when we grew up. I wrote that I wanted to be an astronaut. I was told that girls couldn't be astronauts. I should think about being a stewardess."*

Barbara was born in a small town in the rural South. During the years when the turmoil over racial integration first began to erupt, her father entered the Christian ministry. From that point on, Barbara describes her childhood as deeply religious with a focus on social and political issues, "I always had the sense of being morally and ethically different from everybody else." When the time came to leave home for college, she chose a small church-related college affiliated with her father's denomination and planned a career in religious education. She fulfilled the expectations of her parents throughout college and, again, as a teacher following graduation.

Barbara recalls, "There was a period when I thought about becoming a missionary but instead I took a teaching position in a super-conservative small town in Virginia. I hated living there, hated the constraints, and hated being criticized by older teachers who thought my skirts were too short and my hair was too long. I would come home from school every night and cry, and

I'd get sick every Sunday. After the first year, the school board decided not to renew my contract. I felt rejected, but at the same time I was relieved. A few days later, I saw a Peace Corps poster at the post office. It said, 'Ask not what your country can do for you…' So I walked straight up to the window and asked for an application.

"I had no idea what I was letting myself in for. I requested French West Africa because I had studied French in college. They asked me if I'd consider going to Thailand to teach English. I said, 'Thai-where?' My parents said, 'Isn't that near Vietnam?'" The Peace Corps period was *the* central turning point in Barbara's life. "I broke out of all the constraints and family values of home, and for the first time, I had the opportunity to get to know myself away from all those things that I had always thought were me. I discovered almost immediately that many of the things that I thought were important were not. One of the metaphors I used again and again was that I felt like an onion with the layers being peeled away, and I just kept peeling until I found the real me."

She completed her two year service in 1973 and became engaged to a Jewish man she met in the Peace Corps. Because Barbara came from a strictly Christian background, she was quite uncertain about what her family was going to think. Barbara and her fiancé decided that if anyone didn't like it, they would just thumb their noses in the face of the world. She wrote her parents and said, "We want a very small wedding, no fuss, no parties." Her parents said, "You can't do that! You can't invite your family and friends and not entertain them properly!" At that time, all over the country, young couples were exchanging wedding vows barefoot in the park. Correspondingly, Barbara had little interest in a big white wedding.

"I had my wedding dress made in Thailand out of Thai silk. It was very severe, just an A-line dress with a mandarin collar and long sleeves. That was it, as simple as possible. I airmailed it back to the states. When I got off the plane, the first thing my mother said to me was, 'I saw your wedding dress and I cried.' I thought, 'Uh-oh. I think we have a conflict of values here.' I came face to face with the fact that my life had transformed and that I had changed from my family irreparably. They saw the whole thing as a rejection of their values which was very difficult for them to deal with. All I could see was that my world had expanded and it seemed to me that this was a good thing. In any event, I wore my dress and we went ahead with all their plans. At the end of my wedding day, my mother said to me, 'You were beautiful.' "

New Truth: Honor your traditions but act on what you think is right.

For many women of this generation, their individual interests and abilities developed as they encountered pivotal choice points. Much to their surprise, they found that life did not progress through a predetermined sequence of stages. Barbara found herself without a teaching position and decided spontaneously to apply for the Peace Corps. Although Barbara saw her opportunities increasing and her self-awareness growing, her parents looked at their much-changed daughter and felt her behavior was a repudiation of their values. Interestingly, when we asked Barbara why her life turned out as it had, she answered,

"My parents. They made me the person I am. They taught me not to live my life according to the mores of the world, which ironically made me do things that have hurt them very deeply." She believes that if her parents thought about this, they would probably agree.

A number of women of this generation have spent some period of their lives alienated from one or both of their parents. In Barbara's case, when she converted to Judaism, she and her family did not speak for several years. After she and her father resumed contact, he told her, "I always taught you to do what you thought was right. If you think this is right, then this is what you have to do." Some women selected options that were painful for their parents to accept. Now that she is a parent herself, Barbara has a greater understanding of this dilemma.

Separating From the Past

> "Life is unpredictable. Even if you follow all the rules, it doesn't mean you're going to get rewarded in the end, so you might as well test out the waters. That's what I figure."

The breaking away period for the women we interviewed taught them two important life lessons: first, that they could take risks and second, that they had options. For the first time, they saw there were new paths to follow—they could have a real career, be intimate but not get married, reject set ways of thinking, and follow their instincts. Above all, they realized they could have their own identity, separate from a man, which could be defined, shaped, and molded by their own choices. Unlike women of previous generations, they had a taste of freedom at a pivotal point in their young adult development. As one woman said, "My clearest aspiration was to get out of town. Once I got out and could begin to explore the world on my own terms, I knew I'd figure it out." This spirit of independence, optimism, and spirit characterized countless accounts that we heard.

The stories in this chapter also show how complex, circuitous, and individualistic the actual processes are by which women begin to come into their own. Moving from adolescence to young adulthood involves separating from parents, choosing a career path, and formulating a sense of identity. For most women of this generation, completing these developmental milestones was more complicated and challenging. The process took longer than it did for their older sisters and mothers because they were developing intimacies, defining careers, and forming identities that would continue to evolve throughout their lives.

Chapter Three

I was a Foot Soldier in the Sexual Revolution

A Truth Seeker visits a wise guru who lives in a cave at the top of a mountain and asks, "What is the secret of life?" The guru says, "Good judgment." She thinks about that and says, "How does one get good judgment?" The guru says, "Through experience." The Seeker asks, "How does one get experience?" The guru says, "Bad judgment."

"Many of those who carried the torch got first degree burns."

—Carolyn Kizer, poet

Sex, Drugs, and Rock and Roll

Torchbearer women were exposed to an expanded and more delicious world than their mothers had known. While the primary lesson learned during the breaking away years was not to be fearful, the trade-off was the loss of both protection and predictability. Some women were swept away, at least temporarily, by the freedom of the times; others were caught up in the extremes and excesses that accompanied the major social changes going on in America. What happened to the women who went too far, too fast? What temptations or ideals led them astray? How did they regain control over their lives? These women, who did more than taste the forbidden fruit, learned from their experiences with drugs, alcohol, promiscuity, and extreme political activism. Eventually, they recaptured their physical, psychological, and emotional balance.

The pivotal events of the late 1960s, including the Chicago riots, Summer of Love, Kent State, and Woodstock provided fertile opportunities for young women who were more than ready to break out, explore, and experiment. Hundreds of thousands of women, raised under "nice girls don't..." prohibitions, were ripe for both a personal and ideological rebellion. Timothy Leary's words, "Turn on, tune in, drop out!" played out in stark contrast to the repressive messages of the '50s. In this relatively guilt-free environment, young women found themselves behaving in ways they would not have thought possible a few months earlier. Their youthful willingness to try new things and take big chances blurred the age-old distinction between nice and not-so-nice girls so that by the time the '60s ended, nice girls had done some pretty wild and dangerous things.

As a group, this generation overcame fears of deviating from the norm—of seeming different, being alone, or standing out rather than fitting in—and began to take risks. Guided by the unofficial credo, "If it feels good, do it," some women became enmeshed in the taboo and the tempting. Naturally there were excesses, and for some, the lines between use and abuse, between risk and real danger, and between legitimate protest and subversive activities were crossed.

When their behaviors led to the more sordid aspects of life, including the illegal, the immoral, and the perilous, the taste proved bittersweet. A successful artist describes her experience during this period, "For the first time in my life, I was turned loose in the world. That whole period was very dark. Some thought it was liberating, but I found it disconcerting. I was swept into the world of open sexuality and easily available drugs. I wasted a lot of time being with the wrong men in the wrong places. Half the time I was incoherent, so I missed a great deal of what was going on. I'm lucky to be alive considering some of the things I did."

Although risks were taken, of the women we interviewed, no lives were irreparably ruined. Some women went through a period of psychological bungee jumping—hurling themselves off the edge, swinging in space, and then bouncing back. While there were some significant life-saving turn-arounds, many simply got bored, met new people, or created alternatives that brought them back into the mainstream. By then, the world had changed and they returned from marginal lifestyles to a different environment.

Women of this generation were taught from an early age that if they made a mistake or deviated from parental injunctions, their lives and their reputations would be damaged forever. Yet, many women learned that they could come back to themselves and their core values, even after making extreme or bad choices. Although they didn't know how things would turn out, their optimism and belief in their own basic goodness enabled them to move forward in the tasks of regrouping, recovering, and rebuilding their lives. When all was said and done, new strategies of self-reliance were discovered when they drew on their inner power and strength. By bouncing back and reclaiming themselves, they accomplished the developmental task of breaking away, giving new meaning to the word "resilience" in the process, and illuminating new principles for living that would stand them in good stead in the future.

Old Rule: Parents are all good, all powerful, and all knowing.

"When I was growing up, I was forbidden to do anything. Every time I wanted to try something new, my mother would go into a tirade of all the horrible possibilities that might happen. As soon as I was free, I jumped into the fire. I tried everything imaginable. I met the seediest people and went to the seediest places. I wanted to see the dark side. Unless I knew the dark side, I couldn't reject it, speak with the voice of authority, and make choices about how to live my life."

Blessed with a keen mind and an intellectual curiosity well beyond her years, Sally had a long history of negative encounters with authority figures —beginning with her father, a strict disciplinarian. As a teenager, she was sent to a conservative, rigidly repressive Catholic boarding school where her rebellion and anger grew. After six years at this private girls' academy, Sally was socially unprepared for life at a large coeducational college. She stopped going to class, fell in with marginal people, and started taking drugs in what she called "an attempt to get down to the soulfulness of life." Sally mistakenly thought there was some truth to be found through the use of drugs. Instead, she began to spiral downward.

After a summer in San Francisco, she dropped out of college and married a man of a different race, someone "totally unacceptable to her father" in order to free herself from his control. Not surprisingly, the marriage didn't last. Around the same time, the first anti-sex discrimination laws were enacted, requiring businesses and companies to hire women for nontraditional jobs. Sally was a clerk for the telephone company and she hated it. Her boss urged her to consider outside work. "Two weeks later I was a telephone installer," she says. "It was 1973 and I was the second woman to hold this position. The first was a Playboy bunny who did it for promotional purposes as part of a splashy magazine article about the first women in jobs normally held by men." In her new position, Sally developed social interaction skills, self-confidence, and the ability to perform under stress and to think on her feet. But it was the only pillar of security she had.

Sally, now using drugs heavily, lived in a communal house with six others and began a period of sexual promiscuity. "Everyone had guns and most were dealing drugs. I'd come home during work, drink two vodka tonics, snort a quarter of a gram of cocaine, and go back to work. It was lunacy to the nth degree." She had a list of excuses and justifications a mile long. "I would tell myself that it was OK because it wasn't interfering with my job. Who was I kidding?" Yet, it was her job that kept Sally from sinking into the depths. "I decided I would never put a needle into my vein, but anything short of that I was game for. 'Truth? Where is truth? Let's find it! Maybe it's down this road or after this line.' I had some serious problems."

In retrospect, Sally believes her self-abuse enabled her to feel much like the religious aesthetics who tore themselves apart in order to feel. "When I was young, my parents told me, 'No.' The Church said, 'You can't do that.' I was in a box and had to fight my way out. Unfortunately, I stepped all over myself in order to break free and I stepped over a lot of other people too. The sexual predatory period was an off-shoot of my drug use. I convinced myself that drugs and wild behavior were the road to well-being. By learning about myself with such intensity, I thought I could finally plumb the depths of my emotions and wrench from my frozen past a semblance of feeling, emotion, and passion. I didn't have the wisdom to see that I could do it without the aid of stimulants."

The voice of reason spoke out one day when Sally, at home with an illness, observed two of her drug partners. As she watched them get high, Sally realized she was kidding herself into thinking this was the truth and the passion that she'd been seeking. "I was living the biggest lie of all," she says. "What I thought was friendship was really mutual self-abuse. Once my so-called friends realized I was serious, they never darkened my door again."

New Truth: Find the power within and use it.

Sally emerged from this chaotic period stronger and wiser. One day, while returning to her truck after installing some telephone equipment in a dangerous part of town, she noticed three men moving towards her in a menacing way. "These guys embodied negative energy. There was no one around. A horrible feeling came over me like a wave. I knew enough about life on the street to realize that they saw me as an instant victim. My truck was boxed in. I couldn't get out. They surrounded the truck and I began to tremble, saying, 'God, what am I going to do?'

"I thought, 'Go down to the depths and bring out the beast.' I felt myself draw up as savage energy flowed through my body. My being was transformed. One guy had his face pressed against the driver's window. I leaned back in the seat, turned sideways, stared right at him, and let out the most unearthly sound I've ever heard. He fell back writhing on the cement, screaming to the others, 'Get away! She's crazy.' My whole body was pulsing and I could have torn his eyes out if I had to. To this day, I have no idea where that power came from. Perhaps I would not have been able to find the strength to tap into that kind of energy if I hadn't been around seedy people, had some insane experiences, and been through so much." By relying on her instincts, Sally was able to muster incredible courage in the face of danger and act in a most decisive, empowering way.

Sally, with her long history of rebellion against authority, discovered her own power when she stopped directing her energy toward external targets. The quest to be her own person, free from parental and societal control, shifted to rebellion against accepted norms and standards in young adulthood. Her abuse of drugs and alcohol represents the path she took in her search for self. She says, "I used to think of myself as a sponge, wanting to get saturated with an experience so I could feel it, breathe it, and be it. Only then could I evaluate the experience honestly. I'm not someone who can stand back, look at something from a distance, and expect to know it. I can't feel an elephant's trunk and say I know what an elephant is. I want to get inside the elephant's skin. Then I can tell all you about elephants."

The issue for Sally was very basic: Who am I? She had to come to terms with her personal power to answer that question. Sally had to break all the rules before discovering that the freedom she was seeking to gain by rebelling could only be found within. When she began to act in her own best interest, instead of acting out against authority, she was able to access the untapped, powerful energy within and get back on track.

Well before women were writing about seeking their "Wild Woman nature," women of this generation were finding and confronting the hidden parts of themselves. Risk-taking and rebellion beyond accepted limits had consequences—including alternative lifestyles, malevolent strangers, and danger. Young women like Sally found themselves in situations where they had to follow their instincts and intuition in order to survive. At the same time, they also were filling their reservoirs of experience and solidifying their sense of self to draw on later in life.

Old Rule: A man defines a woman's identity.

"As women, we have been trained to ignore our gut feelings, listen to others, and distrust what we believe if it conflicts with societal values. Looking back, I'm surprised at how incredibly on-the-spot my instincts were. When I didn't listen, I got into trouble every damn time."

The little girl who was once a girl scout, a school office monitor, and a youthful Goldwater volunteer lived out her parents' worst nightmare between the ages of fourteen and twenty-four. Carla spent many years homeless and lost. As a flower child, she lived a marginal existence and worked only occasionally as a bartender and waitress. After a series of abusive relationships with men, she became depressed and suicidal. Reflecting on that period of her life, Carla concludes, "I took the hard road.

"I started using drugs in high school and kept taking them until I had given everything up. By the time I was nineteen, I was living in garages, abandoned buildings, and alleys. I was in a horrible relationship with a crazy man who believed we could get whatever we wanted by going through peoples' garbage and taking what they wasted."

Carla felt totally lost a year later when this relationship fell apart. She considered suicide, but "I couldn't kill myself because I knew that would destroy my mother. Ironically, I value that time in my life because it showed me how low a person can go. I went through such a deep, dark tunnel that I wasn't afraid anymore. Slowly, I began to come out of my depression. I knew I couldn't do hallucinogens or smoke marijuana again, and I didn't want to drink. I began doing Tai-Chi and karate and taking sensible care of my body. But, unfortunately, I traveled the hard road again. I took a job in a bar because the money was good."

Carla soon became dependent on alcohol. "Suddenly, I wasn't shy anymore; I was vivacious and able to loosen up," she remembers. "I actually thought that if I went to bed with a man, that meant he loved me. Later, I would find out that he was married or had a girlfriend. My life revolved around men and my role was to serve them. Some guy would call me up at 3 A.M. and say, 'Honey, come on over,' and I'd be right there. Eventually, I realized I was nobody to these men and that I was being used. I felt like a prostitute."

New Truth: Only *you* can define your self-worth.

Carla was living at the time with a group of women in a house they jokingly called the Venus Fly Trap "because so many men came and went." One day, she had a moment of incredible clarity. Carla looked at herself in the mirror and said, "'No more!' Clear as a bell, I knew I had to get out of that life. With a very different consciousness, I worked for one more month. I became angry when I began to see the amount of manipulation and game playing that was going on. I watched men trying to use me or other women, but they couldn't touch me anymore. I saved up some money, quit my job, and left for Hawaii."

Carla realized on a personal level what the women's movement was all about. "I didn't spend a lot of time reading Ms. magazine because I wasn't a feminist or in a career at that point. I was doing a lot of gut-heart living. Women were forming consciousness-raising groups, but my whole life revolved around drinking, doing cocaine, and the 'rich guy is the better guy' scene. Even though I was doing a lot of self-destructive things, some part of me was always saying, 'This isn't you. This isn't something you have to keep doing.' When I look back, I can see that my world depended on my relationships with men. After I got to Hawaii, I asked myself, 'Who am I?' I realized that relationships with men had to begin with who I am, not with who they needed me to be."

Many women go through a period when they are unsure of their identity and, like Carla, find a sense of self and belonging through involvement with men. Adapting and making themselves fit into someone else's life structure, they look to others for direction and sometimes drift into compromising and dangerous situations. Sooner or later, a woman must face herself, discover her intrinsic value, and make respectful personal choices if she is to develop successfully into adulthood. After drifting aimlessly for years, Carla confronted the underlying issue of her own self-worth. In essence, she had to go down to come up.

Like many women who had extended or traumatic breakaways from their families, Carla's career direction didn't emerge until after she changed her destructive lifestyle. Before that, she worked at odd jobs primarily to survive rather than to receive validation for her capabilities. Carla regrouped from her period of excess and built a new life. From her new position of strength, she was able to weather a terrible loss—the death of her child—and later to develop her unique, creative talents into a successful design business.

Old Rule: Nice girls live up to parents' and society's ideals for women.

"Define yourself. Allow no one, nothing to define you, except what comes from within. Be your own counsel. Once you allow someone else or some standard to define you or guide your behavior, you deny everything that you can be. It's a self-induced paralysis that will speed your demise faster than any illness or accident that could befall you."

After graduating from college Cum Laude in math, Denise became engaged to her high school sweetheart. Before she got married, Denise had a passionate affair that marked the start of her personal rebellion. When she realized she was pregnant, she had an abortion seventeen days after the procedure became legal in New York. Denise felt a deep sense of discontent about her pre-ordained future. She didn't want to be a high school teacher or get married, but felt she didn't have whatever it would take to get out. Her wedding was a miserable experience. "We had a Jewish ceremony and the groom has to break the glass by stomping on it. Right before the ceremony my husband said, 'I'm not doing it!' I said, 'Please, break the glass. Don't ruin the wedding.' I remember hating him and being very upset. This was the start of a very bad marriage."

Denise and her husband moved to a large East Coast city where she worked for the courts. "There was a whole department of investigators, most of whom were men. That's when my sexual revolution started," Denise says. "I had an affair with one of the investigators. I wasn't in love with him, but I used the affair as a way to end the marriage. My husband threatened suicide. We went to therapy together but it was over for me. This was not what my very conventional parents wanted for their daughter. There had never been a divorce in my family. After that, I became very promiscuous, dating lots of other men. I started drinking but I didn't do drugs yet."

Obsessed with her weight, Denise developed a serious eating disorder, using binge eating and fad diets. At the same time, she renewed contact with a woman she had known as a teenager who wanted to move to California. Denise thought, "That will solve my problems. I was going to become a singer and she wanted to write the Great American novel. We sold all our things, stuffed our prized possessions in her little Fiesta, and drove off for lands unknown. But this woman had problems too. She taught me the trick of bulimia and she was also a drinker. To this day, I don't know how we made it across the country alive. We drank in the car and stayed with strangers. We were both raped. It was an out-of-control period. I was smoking, drinking, having sex with everybody, and binging and purging—I was a twenty-three-year-old mess."

Once in California, her friend became homesick and left. Denise stayed and got a job as a cocktail waitress at a go-go club. "I fell for a crazy musician who liked having group sex—three-ways, four-ways, stuff like that. My bulimia was more serious than ever and I used opium, heroin, and speed. I became very sick and made two suicide attempts. I lived like this for three years. Eventually, I was hospitalized with gastritis from throwing up so much and ingesting too much aspirin. I had a tubal pregnancy, a miscarriage, and several abortions. I also developed a constipation problem because I used laxatives to push food through my system."

After spending so much time in the hospital, Denise began a training program to become a nurse. She couldn't handle it because she was still too sick. It was at this point that she met her husband, the man who saved the day. "One day, I was looking at a double rainbow and crashed my car into a Lincoln Continental. It was completely my fault. In the emergency room, the doctor who was treating me asked, 'Are you hurt?' I said, 'No.' He said, 'Good. That's all that's important.' There was a calmness in his voice and chemistry right in that moment. And that's how we met."

But Denise's life didn't turn around immediately. "I was still up to a lot of my old tricks. Even through the first year or two of our marriage, I was consuming drugs and still bulimic." She had her epiphany when she discovered dancing. "Disco was really popular and the movie *Saturday Night Fever* was playing everywhere. We went to a club and were watching this couple dance. I said, 'I have to do this.' I don't remember anything else in my life that was ever as clear. I was twenty-seven and had never danced before in my life, but that was the start of my dancing career and the end of my self-destructiveness."

New Truth: Nice girls can screw up and still be nice girls.

Denise was tired of being sick and living on the edge. She says, "I always knew I was a good person." At age thirty she began EST training, an experience that was to change her way of thinking about herself. "It was a big revelation for me to learn that I had something to do with how my life turned out. For some reason I never had gotten that. I thought things were just happening to me. The training clicked and I started taking responsibility for my life."

Denise's story represents the excesses and extremes that affected some of the women in her generation. After years of following her parents' wishes and trying to meet external standards, she ended a bad marriage and rebelled against all convention. Denise had many sexual relationships and developed multiple addictions. Her issues related to food, combined with the opportunities for excess in her environment, left her vulnerable. She was running on empty until she discovered her passion for dance and came to realize her own worth. When she began to exercise personal control, Denise was able to overcome her addictions, establish long-term relationships, and create a successful career.

Old Rule: Accept the status quo.

"I was looking for drama. I had a vision of the way things ought to be and tried to make it work in my life. I spent years without a job or income. I had nothing except one suitcase, but I always had a dime in my pocket for a phone call. If I had to use it, I'd bum another one on the street. You don't think about what you're doing or the possible consequences, because the second you do, you get scared."

Much of what went on in the late '60s and early '70s was born out of idealism, rather than personal rebellion. The optimism of the times, reflected in such phrases as "We can be whatever we want to be" or "We can change the world" were felt deeply for the first time. Many young women became disillusioned by the issues facing our country and became involved in efforts to create a more just world. In fact, lifelong commitments to political action and to helping those less fortunate were forged during this time. The stories of Joyce and Vicky, however, illustrate the dangerous and sometimes life-threatening positions some women placed themselves in when their anti-establishment activities went beyond the social norms.

The seeds for Joyce's political radicalism were sown in her childhood years, when she remembers confronting racism and sexism. In her first semester of college she joined the anti-Vietnam War movement, dropped out of school, and became a card-carrying member of the Radical Left. Perhaps it was her solid sense of self and strong personal convictions that enabled her to do what she felt was right. While many of her generation supported the same cause in words, Joyce literally put her life on the line. "Soldiers were being trained and sent to Vietnam. In February 1968, the TET offensive was launched. Vietnam wasn't a little thing anymore," Joyce recalls. "My cousin had been drafted the previous summer. If we didn't do something, there were going to be a lot of young people dying over there. I worked with a group of activists in the anti-war movement who set up coffee houses near military bases. At the time, we got a lot of publicity and the Pentagon even knew about me.

"Many in the peace movement considered G.I.s baby killers. It was our position that the vast majority of soldiers were draftees who were in Vietnam against their will. Because they didn't want to go to jail or to Canada, they decided to do their two years and get out. The purpose of the coffee houses was to give soldiers who were against the war a safe place to go when they were off base. We didn't preach a line, but we did say, 'You can lay down your arms and resist. You don't have to give up your life if you don't want to.' They needed to know that there were other people who felt the same way they did. Our presence told them that there was strength in numbers. We felt that, with proper support, the grunts would stop fighting a ground war and eventually they did. I think that we had a major impact on ending the war. It may have happened without us but I think we helped that process along."

Her involvement with the first coffee house was short-lived because the man she worked with went underground when he got his draft notice. Tom Hayden and Rennie Davis agreed to take over the national leadership of the coffee houses, but they were getting ready for the Chicago Democratic convention in August of '68 and never sent her a replacement. "People threatened to trash the coffee house and beat up the volunteers. I even got shot at. There I was, a naive nineteen-year-old in a basement. I went to see the sergeant-major and asked him, 'Why are you being so mean to the people who come to our coffee house?' I was a very dumb girl!"

Joyce went to the 1968 Democratic convention and then moved to the West Coast to coordinate the coffee house effort at a national level. The FBI came to see her. "They knew I had been in Chicago and wanted to interview me to see if I was guilty of crossing state lines with intent to incite a riot. I would not talk to them. Then, a lawyer who was with the ACLU wrote a letter saying he was going to sue the Army for harassment in my name. I thought, 'Wait a minute! I don't want to sue the Army!' Because there was too much resistance and I was afraid that people might be put in danger, I decided not to open a new coffee house where I was living. By now it was late 1969 and we really thought we were going to make a revolution at any second. I was now working with a group who were connected with the SDS—the Students for a Democratic Society. When they went underground, so did I, but that didn't last very long."

Joyce decided to join the Army to organize soldiers from the inside. In those days a man could enlist at eighteen, but women under twenty-one had to have their parents' permission.

She spoke to her parents and they reluctantly agreed, but she found out later that her father called the FBI and said, "Make sure she doesn't get in." Her father's request was honored.

During this period, Joyce had no roots. She rarely spent more than a month in any one city, but she continued to organize G.I.s, work with military families, and start an anti-war newspaper. Even though she was only in her late twenties, the years of activism were beginning to take a toll and she was ready to move on. Joyce met a conservative, traditional, unpolitical man and fell in love. "I wanted a relationship, but we were very different from each other. My friends asked, 'What do you two talk about?' but somehow there was chemistry between us. I married Stan and we've been together ever since. Saigon fell on April 30, 1977, the day my son was born."

New Truth: Act on your convictions.

Very few American women's lives were untouched by the Vietnam War—many had friends and family members who were drafted, and those who didn't were still affected by the anti-war demonstrations and political unrest that swept across the country. "Questioning authority" became a new way of thinking for many women, whether it related to protesting the war, changing outmoded rules at their universities, or challenging the male establishment. In Joyce's case, her passion to stop the war led to an unconventional lifestyle as a member of the Radical Left, whose identity and choices revolved around the anti-war movement. In the course of living her convictions, she didn't dwell on the potentially volatile and serious consequences of what she was doing, who she was with, or who was watching her every move. Her personal safety was compromised time and again, but she continued to work for what she believed in.

After the war ended, Joyce fell in love, shifted her attention to her new husband and their children, and began living a settled, middle-class life focused on family. But like many women of her generation, she did so with a deep sense of satisfaction, knowing she had been true to herself and had contributed to stopping social injustice.

Old Rule: The government acts in the people's best interests.

"Most college folks use 75 cent words. I just stick with the quarter ones and get the job done."

Vicky was always a tomboy, the only girl in a family of four boys. Growing up, she often heard mixed messages from her parents, "I was always told to get A's, but I wondered, 'Why? What for? To wash dishes, to mow the lawn, to iron shirts, to work in the yard, or to paint the house, I don't need good grades, so why get them?' It was very confusing." Instead of going to college, she chose to work for an insurance company, receiving only a nickel raise after two years. In frustration, she joined the military, becoming one of the first women to work as an electrician on an aircraft.

Like many Torchbearers, Vicky wasn't a rebel. She was never interested in a hippie lifestyle, unlike her brothers. "I saw how hurt, upset, frustrated, and worried my parents were after all my brothers put them through." How could this young, conservative woman who never quite fit in as a child, but who blossomed and came into her own in the military, become a drug carrier?

Vicky received many promotions throughout her exemplary military career, but then chose to leave the military because of her anger over self-serving government practices. Congress had just voted itself a large pay increase, but had denied an increase to the military. Instead, military personnel like herself were told they were eligible for food stamps. The issue became a moral one for Vicky. "Can you imagine defending your country and being told to apply for food stamps? Our pay was a mere pittance and we had been denied raises. I experienced serious anger for the first time in my life over this issue," she remembers.

Vicky's disillusionment escalated when a military plane she was flying in suddenly lost an engine and the crew had to make an emergency landing on an unknown island in the Mediterranean. "We opened the door and I saw this guy with an M16 pointed right at me. It was the scariest moment in my life. I was the only person he'd let off the plane because I was a female. I had to fix the airplane all by myself. Thank God I was there, because the crew didn't think he would have let a man get off." Her rationale for becoming a smuggler had its roots in this experience. "I was the one who had to stand there and look down the barrel of that gun, not members of Congress, and I had others' lives on the line, too," she told us.

A second experience contributed to the growing gap between her idealism and reality. "We had just finished loading a cargo plane with military gear," she says, "when I saw a huge cart come out on the tarmac full of golf clubs! We were knowingly ordered to overload the plane to pack up those clubs. Then we fueled up the tanks to the max because we were going to Cuba where you can't refuel." She later found out the golf clubs belonged to some Congressmen who were ostensibly traveling on government business. Before the plane took off, Vicky remembers telling the pilot the plane wasn't balanced and he would have to handle the lift-off differently.

As the plane lifted, they literally ran into a thousand sea gulls. "We lost an engine because of the birds. Blood was everywhere," she recalls. "The pilot got on the instrument panel, started pulling, and said, 'We're going to die.' If we were to land, we'd lose our struts because we were overloaded and we'd go belly up. We had to keep flying. We flew with our landing gear down all the way to Cuba because we couldn't retract it. We almost died because of those golf clubs. It was really stupid that Congressmen were allowed to override safety issues. I got really angry about being used that way."

After she left the military, Vicky joined the reserves, worked on airplanes and boats, and enrolled in night school. She wasn't part of the Vietnam-era lifestyle that involved drug experimentation or free sex. In her words, "My life was very clean. I would rather fix something than go out and party." But her anger at those Congressmen who were playing golf while people like herself were dying in a war they had declared continued to grow. "My salary was $8,000 the year that Congress voted themselves a huge raise," says Vicky, "and I decided it was time to figure out a way to get back what I felt they owed me.

"As a reservist, I flew regularly to Europe, so I brought marijuana to people I knew who were stationed there in the service. Then I picked up hashish, brought it back, and sold it. I hid the drugs in the wing because I'd always have to go up there to do maintenance work. I had marijuana all over the aircraft. Ironically, I never smoked any of it. I thought of this as getting back what I felt I should have earned, and when I did, I quit."

New Truth: Sometimes you have to confront unjust actions, but you have to be ready to accept the consequences.

If Vicky had been born in a different era, she would not have engaged in a personal battle against the U.S. Congress. She also might not have been in the military or become a drug smuggler either. Her disillusionment and anger towards Congress for not granting raises to the military eventually led her to leave. Vicky broke the law until she "righted the wrong," at least for herself. Now very successful in a technical support field, she lives in the country and espouses generally middle-of-the-road positions.

On opposite sides of the political spectrum, Vicky and Joyce both were motivated by the need to rectify a perceived injustice perpetrated by the government. When Vicky broke away from a low-level local job with few rewards, she took a risk and made an unconventional choice to enter the military, embark on a male-identified career, and travel around the world. At that time, she had no problem with becoming part of the same Establishment that Joyce wanted to subvert.

Both Joyce and Vicky acted in ways that were consistent with their values, even when their convictions put them in extremely precarious situations. But when they accomplished what they felt they needed to accomplish, they moved on and built conventional lives.

Profiting from your experiences

"In the '60s and '70s everything was up for grabs. You could go in any direction or you could go nowhere."

Nice middle-class young women in previous generations had few opportunities to put themselves at risk, so many women of this generation found themselves in uncharted waters with no role models for how to behave when they began to experience freedom and opportunity. Inexperienced and often naive, some engaged in behaviors that were dangerous, damaging, or destructive. Fortunately for them from a developmental perspective, their actions were time-specific and time-limited.

According to psychologist Robert Havighurst, "the teachable moment" is a particularly important time when a person is most ready to learn something new and/or make a major life decision. For the women who got involved excessively with drugs and alcohol, the teachable moment occurred when they stepped back and observed their own destructive behaviors. Then they were able to take the necessary steps to initiate a qualitatively different life. With maturity and increased self-awareness, their motivation and reference group changed and they were able to move on. For the women who reacted to perceived injustices by the system, their risky behavior ended naturally, fortunately without lifelong negative consequences, when they completed what they saw as their respective missions.

The major developmental task of the teens and twenties is to separate from ones' parents, begin to engage in the process of searching for a personal identity, and settle on one that fits. If all went well, young Torchbearer women would become what

Ruthellen Josselson in *Finding Herself* calls "Identity Achievers"—flexible, self-confident women with a sense of purpose who have discovered their inner resources after experimentation and rebellion. The women in this chapter differ from their more cautious risk-taking sisters because they experienced an extended exploratory period that involved at-risk behaviors not socially sanctioned for women (or for men). Yet, they, too, were able to find their sense of purpose and complete the passage into Identity Achiever status before it was too late. Joyce and Vicky actually used this time in their lives to solidify their identities by living their values, even though they put themselves at risk.

Resilience describes the ability to be resourceful and to recover from hardship, adversity, or difficult times. Gail Sheehy in *Pathfinders* wrote, "Women who consistently score at the very top of the well-being scale have suffered just as many hardships and losses as their more miserable contemporaries with one critical difference: they have confronted a difficulty, rocked the boat, picked themselves up, and taken the steps necessary to free themselves from what they perceived as a trap, self-made or imposed." Sally, Carla, Denise, Vicky, and Joyce all have shown remarkable resilience. Having put to rest the old rule that a life could be irrevocably ruined by one bad choice or one mistake, they demonstrated creativity, resourcefulness, and fearlessness in rebuilding their lives. Without exception, they experienced a renewed sense of self and, with that, the courage to go forward and not look back.

Chapter Four

I've Become the Person My Mother Hoped I'd Marry

"In my early fantasies, I had my mother's idea that I would marry a dominant man who would take care of everything and I would be the subordinate person in the relationship. I always looked for men who were stars; they had to be brilliant and accomplished. Instead, I'm the one with the brilliant career. My husband is a down-to-earth, family person. I guess I became the man I wanted to marry."

Baby-boomer women, whether cautious or more extreme risk-takers, became increasingly independent from their families as they moved into their thirties. With a clearer picture of who they were and who they wanted to become, they encountered a new world of options in both love and work. No longer bound by social convention to marry young and have children, they now faced career choices no other generation of women had before. Many women seized upon the opportunities beginning to open for them in the working world. While some had clearly defined career goals, others drifted into professional fields they had never considered.

The Princesses of Serendip

The *Three Princes of Serendip*, a sixteenth-century Persian fairy tale, tells the story of three princes who travel throughout the Orient in search of adventure and romance. In the course of their travels, the young princes made discoveries by a combination of accident and sagacity. Torchbearers, like the Three Princes, have the gift of 'serendipity'—the ability to discover, by chance, things they were not searching for but which they could later capitalize on. In no realm is this more true than in the world of work.

The working lives of the women of this generation are a marked contrast to those of their mothers'. Their mothers, who graduated from college in the 1940s and 1950s, had the lowest rate of employment of any generation of women. In the 1920s, women earned seventeen percent of doctorates and six percent of law degrees; by the regressive 1950s, only ten percent of doctorates and three percent of law degrees were awarded to women and there were fewer women judges, engineers, and college professors than in past decades. In 1902, eight percent of those listed in *Who's Who* were female, but by 1958, less than four percent on the list were female. Sylvia Hewlett, who reports these plummeting figures in *A Lesser Life*, estimates that at that rate of decline, there would be no distinguished American women relative to men in another generation or so.

Only in the last twenty-five years have large numbers of college-educated women prepared for professional careers outside of teaching, nursing, or social work. Three factors enabled college-aged baby-boomer women to reject the traditional female life course model they had grown up believing was their destiny. First, legal abortion and readily available birth control assured reproductive freedom which no other generation had ever known. Second, in the early 1970s, significant and far-reaching women's rights legislation was enacted, ensuring professional and legal access that had never been available to women before. Finally, as job opportunities were increasing, so was the divorce rate which required a reconsideration about the feasibility of a lifetime of domesticity.

This generation was the first in which great numbers were granted access to the working mainstream and they changed the rules of the American workplace by holding fast to the same high standards and idealistic aspirations they held as 1950s good girls. Today, half of all law students and medical students are women. In 1994, over 80 percent of all female college graduates are in the labor force, most working full-time. Twenty percent of judges, 27 percent of scientists, 20 percent of engineers, 18 percent of state legislators, and 40 percent of Ph.D.s are women. Women own one of every three U.S. firms and are opening new businesses 50 percent faster than men, at a rate of three hundred thousand per year.

Yet, despite considerable achievements, many professional women continue to feel at odds with the male-structured workplace. Although amazing progress has been made, equity has remained an illusive goal chiefly because of how the work environment is organized and domestic responsibilities are allocated. While women have entered top-paying fields, even the most highly educated rise to the top more slowly, less frequently, and make less than men. Says Judith Lichtman, president of the Women's Legal Defense Fund, "We are on faculties, but are not heads of departments. There are very few women who are college presidents or CEOs of Fortune 500 companies. Does discrimination against women still exist because of their gender? Of course." Given the discrepancy between what appears to be tremendous professional mobility and the reality of the glass ceiling, a small "advice and inspiration" industry for working women has been generated in the form of magazines, how-to trade books, and networking groups.

If women were more comfortable in the corporate and professional world, they would not be spending their time and money learning how to behave, dress, and communicate at work. Because of the alien culture of the workplace, and the sharp differences between themselves and prominent men in the same field, many women tend not to see themselves as particularly successful or as matching the stereotype of someone in their profession. The absence of rules, mentors, and well-defined career ladders have led many women to view themselves as achieving their goals by default rather than because of conscious planning. In this context, the women of this generation made serendipitous choices that reflect a negotiation between fortuitous opportunities and active attempts to make sense of and respond to them. Yet, it is the very absence of rules and role models for professional women which compelled them to invent new and effective principles for the workplace.

Like the Princes of Serendip, the women in this chapter base their professional success on both their aptitude for making fortunate discoveries and their hard work, drive, and creativity. Two criteria must be met to discern something as serendipitous. First, the discovery must be of something not sought, and second, it must be capitalized upon by talent and wisdom. Their stories illustrate how they had the knack of spotting and exploiting unanticipated and unforeseen good things while searching for something else. Their journeys—the detours, false starts, and obstacles—describe how these women forged careers and succeeded without clear career paths, role models, or even the conviction that they deserved to be outside the narrow sphere generally reserved for women. Based on the serendipitous discoveries they made, what principles did they create to replace the old rules?

Old Rule: Marry a doctor, don't be one.

> *"I have always been a risk taker and I always will be. Yet, I don't act impulsively. I think about things for a long time, wait for the right opportunity, and then, when the time is right, I do it."*

We were very excited about meeting Dr. Julie because we thought that we were going to interview someone who knew exactly what she wanted to do professionally from an early age. We expected her career history to reflect a straight progression from a college major in pre-med through medical school to a residency in her specialty—in other words, a lifelong focus on becoming a kidney transplant surgeon. Nothing could be further from the case. In fact, we have met only a handful of women in this age group whose career trajectories parallel those of men.

As a child, Julie considered herself artistically inclined. She chose academics because when she did well in school, she was rewarded by not being hit by her father. She recalls, "I never really thought about a career until I had to pick a major in college. I thought I might try pre-med but I was much happier in the liberal arts courses." After college, she spent three years in graduate school studying psychology. Although an excellent student, her professors warned her that she was going to have a hard time finding a job in a geographic area where she would like to live. Julie began to wonder, "Why am I going through this to either end up in Oklahoma or with no job at all?" Terrified at the thought of being unable to support herself, and realizing that she didn't want to be dependent on anyone, especially her father, she began taking her career seriously.

She recalls, "I applied to medical school, but, in the early '70s, it was not easy to get accepted if you were a woman. At that time, only 8 percent of all medical school students were female. A woman had to be something really special and I wasn't, or I didn't think I was. I didn't have a Ph.D. or multiple publications. My father wasn't a physician or somebody of that stature. I applied to many medical schools and got rejected by all of them."

Julie heard about programs in Europe for Americans who didn't get into medical school in the United States. She'd always wanted to learn French, so she enrolled in medical school in Paris. In Europe, students begin studying medicine right after high school. Most of the students were seventeen or eighteen and Julie was twenty-five. "It was incredibly difficult and the language was impossible," she remembers. "I literally spent the first two months not understanding one word in class so I stopped going to lectures. I needed time to learn French. I went to the study halls and worked on my own. One day, all of a sudden, everything made sense. I understood nothing and then I understood everything. After that, school was a breeze."

That April, Julie's mother sent her a *New York Times* article about a new medical school and urged her to apply. Julie completed an application just to humor her mother. At the end of her first year, she found out she had been accepted. Julie ultimately chose to return to the U.S. because she was tired of being discriminated against as a female and as a foreigner, plus, she was older. Everybody talked her into going back, although it is something she has always regretted. She says, "I'm sure I could have pulled off staying in Paris somehow, but, at the time, I didn't have the courage."

Julie finished medical school and began a residency program where she had a surgical fellowship with a subspecialization in the kidney. She had it all planned but then she met her future husband. He was moving to Colorado and convinced her that she should give up the fellowship and go with him. She did. "I figured that I could continue my studies anywhere, but when I got there, they didn't have internal medicine fellowships which I qualified for. I ended up as a general practitioner at an HMO where I was miserable. Several years later, I met the chief of internal medicine at a local hospital. He couldn't pay me, but I was so desperate that I worked for free. Ultimately, because of his own guilt, he paid me a salary of $10,000 a year. I was thirty-one when I got married and thirty-three when my son was born. I started the internal medicine fellowship when I was thirty-four

and finished when I was thirty-six. I still hadn't done the necessary training, so my mentor arranged for me to train in Pitts-
burgh, Chicago, and Los Angeles. I finished the training just
before I turned forty."

Today, Julie is the chief of the kidney transplant program at
a large private hospital. She is finally doing what she was trained
to do. As she looks back at her life, she appreciates her tenacity
and willingness to persevere in the pursuit of her dream. "Paris
was about coming to terms with myself and the past," she says.
"I enjoyed that time so much. Even doing the laundry was an
experience! My brain was working overtime, but it was an
incredible period. You don't realize you have the capacity to do
all the things you can do until you're challenged. It is remarkable what a woman can do!"

New Truth: You are capable of having any career you want.

Torchbearers did not grow up in a culture that said to young
girls, "You have a career ahead of you—you can be a doctor or a
lawyer or anything else you want to be." As children and ado-
lescents, their orientation towards future work was quite different from the one laid out for baby-boomer boys. Serendipitously,
because Julie was born and raised during a period of relative
prosperity, elevated educational standards, and widespread optimism, she was well-equipped to enter the professional gateways
when they opened to women in the 1970s.

Like many women who were among the first to enter pre-
dominantly male professions, Julie did not plan her career the
way men her age did. Julie was twenty-five when she began her

medical studies, although she laid the groundwork by taking a Bachelor of Science degree and completing her pre-med requirements. Once Julie decided to take the plunge and enter medical school she faced two formidable challenges—acclimating herself to an unfamiliar culture and mastering a foreign language. Few male physicians followed such a circuitous route to reach their professional goal and have the mettle and forbearance to follow it for twenty years! Julie is truly someone who succeeded by virtue of sheer persistence. But the most striking theme in her story is her need to take control of her career. Although she tried to play a supporting role in her husband's life script, she soon realized this was a false part.

Julie, like many women her age, is not driven by her professional success or the desire to earn enormous sums of money. The mother of a busy pre-teen, Julie speaks of cutting down on her successful practice, or leaving it altogether, in order to enhance her own personal development. Although her potential for even greater financial rewards is high, Julie places greater value on work that she finds intrinsically rewarding, socially useful, and contributes to her personal development. She speaks of donating her services in Third World countries. "All they have to do is give me a place to stay," she says. Clearly Julie is someone for whom money does not represent independence. She told us, "I won that in my twenties and thirties."

Old Rule: Men make the money, women make the coffee.

"I tell my female employees what no one ever said to me, 'You are capable. Anything is possible. Don't be intimidated, especially by men who try to bully you. You will

succeed. It's just a matter of time until you get more experience.' "

Despite an impoverished childhood, a lack of formal education, and a long history of poorly paid menial employment, Minna is president of her own company and earns $175,000 a year. Along the way, she faced two issues which are hardly unusual for women of her generation: first, that marriage to the prince on a white horse might not happen so she better take care of herself and, second, that support from other women is as critical in the workplace as it is in one's personal life.

Her parents divorced when she was seven. As a result of that major upheaval, Minna's mother moved her three children from a lovely house in the country to a one-bedroom apartment in downtown Salt Lake City. Four family members shared one bed; two slept on the mattress and two on the box spring. Because her mother was either working or sleeping, the burden of cooking, cleaning, ironing, and handling practical matters fell on the children. Minna recalls, "At the ripe old age of seven, I said to myself, I'll never depend on a man for my financial security."

When she graduated from high school in 1968, Minna enrolled at a local business school. The first day, a classmate named Norm asked her what she was doing there. She said she was there to learn computer programming. He told her she would never make it, "You're a woman. Computers are about logic and everyone knows that women are not logical." From that instant forward, Minna's success was assured—there was no way she was going to fail that course. At graduation, Minna and Norm were both hired by the same computerized ticket company. The first day on the job, as she walked past his desk toward the key punch machine, Norm handed her his program and said, "Key punch these for me." Unsure how to respond, Minna said the first thing that came to mind, "Go to hell!" Eventually she gained his respect, but she felt she had to earn it every inch of the way.

Although Minna liked making her own money and living away from her family, she assumed the work was temporary. "I was the typical female in that I thought some guy would marry me and rescue me from my low-level job," Minna says. "I worked as a programmer for four years until I got so bored that I lied my way into an office clerk job. They asked me, 'Can you use a ten key?' I said, 'Of course.' I didn't even know what a ten key was. Within three months, I was office supervisor. I stayed there for a few years until I realized that I was working ten hours a day and making only seven hundred dollars a month. I decided that the real money was in sales."

Minna's next job was selling visual aids to people who were legally blind. Minna felt that this job had an up-side because the product was helping people, but she was still making only nine hundred dollars a month. Her next job was selling dictating equipment. Minna kept struggling to find the right product. When she was twenty-nine, she asked herself, "Where am I going?" It shocked her that she had no plan for her life on the brink of turning thirty.

During that time, Minna was approached by an organization called Women in Sales. The purpose of this group was to help women who never held paid jobs to integrate into the working system. They were taught how to write resumes, how to dress, and how to interview. Women in Sales also served as a network for sharing information about job opportunities. The feminist movement was well-established at that point, but the idea of women networking together was quite new. Working women were finally learning where to turn—to each other, which is what they'd always done anyway.

"Through that group, I learned about a sales position in the carton industry," Minna says. "I became very good at selling, but I still had this typical female loyalty to the company. I stayed there ten years even though they were giving other people promotions and additional territories. Five years ago, I decided that there was no reason to tolerate that treatment any longer. I started my own company and took my clients with me. I faced a very tough lawsuit. The president of the company threatened me, 'I'm going to sue you. I have millions of dollars at my disposal. I'm going to call your customers and drum you out of the business.'

"The more he tried to intimidate me, the less I was willing to back down. My position was that these were my clients although his position was that the customers were his property. I told him there was enough market for everybody, but he felt I was setting a bad precedent. In fact, while I was the first woman to ever break away from the company, several men left to start their own businesses and they never had been threatened or sued. It was a situation where a man was trying to intimidate and bully a woman into getting what he wanted. My response was, 'I was a model employee for ten years. I generated millions of dollars for you and now you want to turn me into a bag-lady?' I took him on and now I'm making six figures."

New Truth: Count on other women for support and guidance.

Many women felt a strong sense of isolation and discomfort when they entered male-dominated professions, so they began to build networks to provide the advice and mentoring support previously unavailable. Minna continues to be actively involved in women's business organizations. The new "Old Girl's Network" has taken hold in virtually every community and professional field. These new groups are extensions of previous female support strategies such as consciousness raising and friendship circles.

In *New Passages*, Gail Sheehy reports the results of a recent survey on the confidence level of American women: "Across the board women felt more independent and sure of themselves... but it was the movers and shakers of the median age forty-one who displayed the highest level of confidence of all." Minna was forty-one when she started her own company and learned that she could take care of herself. When asked about the central issues in her life however, Minna told us, "Definitely not my career! I worked very hard to get where I am, but my emphasis has shifted." Like many baby-boomer women who always seem to be in the process of change, Minna is already thinking about her next "career." She expects her next commitment to be in the area of spiritual and healing practices.

"I was dealt a set of cards at my birth," she says. "I played those cards the best way I knew how. It could have turned out better, it could have turned out worse, but it turned out the way it did. There's a certain aspect to life that's destiny. Some things you have total control over and some parts of life you only have some control over. I've made mistakes but I've done some things right. It's just been God and me."

Old Rule: Girls can't play with the big boys.

> *"When I was in my first year at the law firm, I signed up for the basketball team because I love basketball. I practiced and went with the team to our first game. When I got there a referee said, 'What are you doing here? You can't play. Our insurance policy doesn't cover women. The contract to use these courts is just for men.' My teammates played without me. I was enraged. I wrote the Lawyers' Basketball League saying it's unconstitutional to have a contract with the city for only men to play basketball. Then came the really horrible part. One of my male colleagues said, 'How dare you challenge this practice? We have such a lovely relationship with this referee and the basketball league and here you are making trouble.' I felt betrayed but I continued to hammer away and changed the rules."*

Some may think the word Torchbearers was coined to describe women such as Ellen, a successful attorney, a loving wife, and busy mother of two. Ellen had a conventional East Coast middle-class upbringing which was very much oriented toward education. She was expected to get a terrific education, get married, have kids, and, if necessary, work as a teacher. But the message that she was supposed to do well academically, then just stop and get married, didn't make sense, "If I was supposed to succeed, then I should succeed across the board." The most compelling aspect about Ellen's childhood was that she had an extremely competent mother who had gone back to work when Ellen was ten. She was always the star employee, but would reject any promotions. When her boss asked her to be office manager instead of office secretary, she regretfully would say, "No, that will conflict with my responsibilities to my family." Seeing her mother unhappy and frustrated made Ellen decide to do things differently herself.

Ellen didn't have a particular career path in mind. When she entered college, she became politically active. She worked as a student coordinator for Senator Robert Kennedy, protested against the war in Vietnam, and during the summers, worked for an Upward Bound program to help inner city youths go to college. "The late '60s were pretty intense," she recalls. "The year I was to graduate from college, the campus had been shut down by student protests. We were supposed to go to this traditional graduation ceremony even though we hadn't been in school for months. The students were told that there would be a signal to leave and go to a counter-graduation being held off-campus. We were in the auditorium and, all of a sudden, a tape recording of Bob Dylan singing 'The Times They Are a-Changing' blasted out. That was the signal. So here's the culmination of four years of college: we hear 'The Times They are a Changing' and we march out. My parents were beside themselves."

Ellen began law school at twenty-one with the idea of changing the world. "Law school was just this unbelievable gift," she says. "At the same time, it was a very challenging experience. There were thirty women out of one hundred fifty students which seems like a small percentage yet, at the time, ours was the first class to ever have that many women. We were rabble rousers. In my last year, there were law firms interviewing on campus that blatantly discriminated against women. We studied Title 7 of the Civil Rights Act which had only been in place for four years and said, 'This doesn't just apply to racial equity—this applies to gender equity too!' As a result, women students filed a discrimination charge against the law school claiming it was an employment agency and that the Civil Rights Act applied to employment agencies."

In the early 1970s, Ellen took a position with a big public interest law firm where she could get good training and experience. Although she loved being a lawyer, she was lonely because only two of the one hundred lawyers in the firm were women. "I'll never forget the law society dinner that I went to my first year with the firm. There were five hundred men and three women. There was no ladies room. They put on a skit which they tried to clean up by taking out all the sexist jokes. That's what it was like then—it was a time of breaking down barriers." After two years, Ellen realized that she would never be comfortable there, so she opened her own law practice with another woman. She immediately felt the difference being in an all-woman environment and not working with men who were always commenting on how she looked. She became very active in feminist matters and represented plaintiffs in civil rights cases. "We were one of the first all-female law firms and were deluged with business. There was a huge market for women lawyers," Ellen remembers.

Meanwhile, Ellen kept looking for Mr. Right. In her early fantasies, she still held her mother's idea of marrying a dominant man who would take care of everything. She looked for men who were brilliant, accomplished, and terrific. "I got married at thirty-three. I met my husband on a blind date. It was love at first sight. My husband is a basic down-to-earth, family-oriented person. I agree with Gloria Steinem's idea that I became the man I wanted to marry. My husband enables me to be who I want to be. I can't imagine having a relationship with a man like myself!"

In her late thirties, Ellen went through many years of infertility treatment, including in vitro fertilization. As someone used to doing whatever she wanted, having complete control, and thinking "if you work at it, you can have it," this was both frustrating and humbling. One day, a lawyer friend called and asked if she would consider adopting a child who was several months old. That afternoon, she and her husband went to his office and met a sixteen-year-old girl and her four-month-old son. They agreed to adopt this child. At the end of the meeting, the lawyer said, "When do you want to do this?" The girl said, "How about tomorrow?" Ellen was completely unprepared. The next day, before she had even bought diapers, she had her first baby at age forty.

"When our son was two, we adopted another baby, a girl. Life is more complicated now. Having children has really impacted the rest of my life. I've become more efficient so I can carve out more time to be with my kids. I'm a computer maniac. I have a laptop and I'm hooked up to my office all the time. My husband is a very devoted father. He works part-time and runs things in the house. This is my family period, although it hasn't affected my career. My life was quite rich before, but now it's just expanded to another horizon."

New Truth: When the rules say you can't play, change the rules.

Twenty-five years ago there were two parallel worlds for men and women. A woman's world was dominated by home and family and a man's by work and professional power. A compelling theme in Ellen's story is her realization that because her competent and talented mother put her family first, she was both frustrated and unhappy. Today, Ellen has an enormously successful law practice as well as a prototypical family. A lot has changed for women, but a lot hasn't. In most marriages with two working parents, wives continue to do 70 percent of the housework. Yet, in Ellen's situation, her husband has reduced his work schedule to parent more fully and enable her to become the major breadwinner, something that would have been unheard of in her mother's day.

Ellen was one of the few women we interviewed who has remained in the same profession for over twenty-five years and one of a handful who entered a male-dominated profession immediately upon graduation from college. Remarkably, she still feels her success is due as much to serendipity as anything. "I'm a person of enormous energy, focus, and drive which explains some of it but a lot is due to luck," she says. "I'm fortunate that I managed to marry a man with whom I'm very compatible and who is an enabler. My life coincided with a lot of social change that was consistent with what was good for me. If I'd had the same interests but had been born ten years earlier, I am certain I would be less happy and satisfied."

Old Rule: Girls are pretty, boys are smart.

"After I gave a report to the Board of Directors, the sole female board member said, 'This is the best presentation we've ever seen.' I left that meeting feeling really good. My boss said, half joking, 'I've been giving presentations for fifteen years and no one ever congratulated me like that. If I hear one more person say what a good job you did, I'm going to scream.' I said, 'Jim, she only said that for female bonding. If you want to borrow my skirt and pumps next time, she'll say the same thing to you.' I think hearing that made him feel better. After that, he didn't feel threatened and he feels threatened by me a lot."

A burglar entered Lia's house while she and her parents were eating dinner. She was held at gunpoint while her parents were locked in a closet. The burglar led her downstairs, she thought, to be raped and murdered. The whole time she kept telling herself, "Don't panic." When he held the gun to her head, she said, "Please do me a favor. If you're going to kill me, take me outside because I don't want my mother to hear this." At that moment, he uncocked the gun and said, "Get a better security system." Then he left. She untied herself and freed her parents from the closet. Clearly her ability to remain cool, calm, and collected during a situation as stressful as this may be one factor which explains her rise from college drama major to international banker.

After fifteen years, half as an accountant with a Big Eight accounting firm and half as a senior bank officer, Lia has tremendous insights about working in male environments. Following more traditional professions of acting and fashion marketing, she has succeeded, as very few women have, in two almost totally male-dominated fields—mergers and acquisitions banking and public accounting. As a senior officer at a major savings and loan financial institution, Lia still looks more like an actress than a banker. Despite the difficulty some managers have accepting her, she has the confidence to be herself rather than fit someone else's picture of who she should be.

Her mother's aspiration for her three daughters was that she wanted them to be happy. Her dad would say, "Happy! What is happy?" He wanted his children to be Emperors. He thought Lia would end up as a lawyer or a criminal; he wasn't sure which. In college, her first major was drama, but in her junior year she switched to clothing and textile retailing.

She recalls, "There was only one retail company I wanted to work for—Nieman Marcus. They were going to interview five thousand college seniors from across the country and pick fifteen for their executive training program. Nineteen seventy-six was a very hard year for employment and a bad year for the economy, so very few companies were coming to campus. Just to get on the interview list, I had to spend the night in line because they were only going to sign up twelve people. The Dean called me in and said, 'You should give up your place because you're not the retail type. You're going to go in there in a homemade dress with your long hair. Nieman's will never choose you.' I told her that I was going to do it anyway. I was the only person in the entire Midwest chosen for their executive program."

Lia became a fashion buyer for junior dresses but found the work neither creative nor intellectually stimulating. She decided to go back to school in order to enter a challenging profession. Since the most challenging course she had taken in undergraduate school was accounting, Lia decided to pursue an MBA in accounting. She finished in a year and one-half. "After graduation, I moved to Dallas because it has five of the Big Eight accounting firms. Initially, I did not like public accounting and I didn't look like an accountant and didn't quite fit in. There were very few women in the firm, but the partner in charge liked me because I wasn't a typical accountant type. Still, the first two years were tough. I didn't do that well in terms of my performance evaluations. When I started managing people, my career took off. Accounting was a different world. I changed planets from where I had thought I was going to be. I realized I wasn't going to be an actress and I wasn't going to be in a creative field. I was in a very technical, male-dominated profession," she explains.

After several years in public accounting, Lia went into banking. Today, she is the head of corporate planning for a sixteen-billion-dollar savings and loan firm. As one of five women in the company at the executive level, she is often the only female present when the top twenty managers in the company meet. She has spent her second career in a field dominated by men, yet, she considers being a woman an advantage. "You are certainly listened to more closely whether it's because they're judging you more harshly or checking you out physically," Lia says. "Your name is certainly remembered more easily. Plus, I dress very femininely and that draws attention. I also have good instincts about people and situations, and how to react and what to say to make someone comfortable or put them at ease, particularly in this environment where male egos are so fragile."

New Truth: Use your femininity as a strength.

Business is still very much a male milieu. Behind all the talk about leveling the playing field and using the talent women and minorities bring to the table, there remains an intransigence when it comes to actually doing so. One persistent hurdle confronted by Torchbearers has been the difficulty of reconciling femininity with feminism on the job, especially with regard to the issue of power. The obvious mismatch between the characteristics associated with femininity (deference, self sacrifice, receptiveness, and harmony) and those necessary for career success (assertiveness, emotional detachment, single-mindedness, and competitiveness) have placed working women in a double bind. Any woman who assumes these "male" attributes runs the risk of being characterized as a "bitch." Attempts to curtail and contain powerful women have led to assaults on public figures, such as First Lady Hillary Rodham Clinton and prosecutor Marcia Clark, as object lessons for others. Those in leadership and professional roles are caught between a rock and a hard place.

Women such as Lia who occupy powerful positions in male-dominated professions had no role models to emulate. Women in a wide range of employment settings during the '70s found themselves outside informal networks for support and guidance. Lia reached the position she holds today without sacrificing her personal style. Yet, she minimizes her obvious competence, at least in front of less-secure male colleagues, to avoid damaging their masculine image when she exercises authority. Lia must act less powerful than she truly is. Perhaps her early drama training has come in handy.

1963 ad for a life insurance company: "Keeping house and caring for the kids fills a woman's day and more. But what if she had to earn a living too? Your wife will never have to face this double duty if you protect yourself."

1977 ad for an airline: "She had breakfast with the national sales manager, met with the client from 9 to 11, talked at an industry luncheon, raced across town to the board meeting, and then caught the 8:05 back home."

As early as 1966, television sit-coms such as *That Girl*, and later, in 1970, the *Mary Tyler Moore Show*, glamorized the plucky single gal living on her own. At the same time, young women were receiving new messages from their peers who were advising them not to rush into marriage and to think instead about becoming self-supporting. But without mentors, role models, and predictable career ladders, exactly how were young women supposed to penetrate occupational environments designed by and for men? Torchbearers have tried to answer this question for thirty years.

Sara Rix, editor of *The American Woman 1990-91*, suggests there are two perspectives on women's recent professional advances, "It's either 'Pilgrim's Progress' or 'The Myth of Sisyphus,' pushing the same rocks up the same hills." Every generation confronts its own set of circumstances and social conditions. Women born between 1945 and 1955 were on the front lines in the early equality battles. Harriet Woods, president of the National Women's Caucus, says, "I am of a generation when women couldn't get financial credit, where there were few women in law schools, engineering, or architecture. The younger generation doesn't remember what came before. They have the after."

The career path for women of this generation is often shaped more like a maze than an arrow. There are several reasons why their work lives have taken such a circuitous course. First, most were not socialized from childhood to see themselves with successful careers. This is not surprising since their mothers' measure of success was to marry a prominent man. Second, many Torchbearers, when asked about their career success, echo *Mad* magazine's Alfred E. Newman's famous comeback, "Who me?" Far too often, they sell themselves short by attributing their achievements to luck ("Gosh, I guess I was in the right place at the right time!"), to being average ("Anyone could have done it."), or to intuition ("I guess I just have good instincts."). In fact, the women of this generation have worked incredibly hard to attain the positions they hold today. The tendency to overdo, while at the same time eschewing credit for one's accomplishments, seems to be a generational trait for those who grew up as 1950s "good girls."

When we ask Torchbearers to explain their success, most answer, "I guess it was luck. I certainly don't remember signing up for this!" Many members of the flying-by-the-seat-of-her-pants generation believe they either drifted into their current professions only to discover they had the appropriate skills or they view themselves as simply having taken advantage of opportunities that materialized along the way. As a result, few take credit for their individual accomplishments or see themselves as noteworthy, even though their actions show them to be very much in control and remarkably effective.

Carly's story is a prime example. She grew up with a naturalist-biologist orientation toward the outdoors. As a child, she and her brothers spent much of their free time exploring the woods and fields near their home. Because she had a strong interest in animals as well as cognitive processes, she knew she would pursue a career studying either dolphins or primates. She began to read everything she could about primates. One book was written by a well-known professor who was teaching at a college thousands of miles away. She recalls, "I decided that I was going to study with him although I had no way to get there and no money for tuition. I went to a transportation service that offered free cars to be driven across the country. I threw everything I owned in the car and landed on the campus with $100 and no place to live.

"I drove to the university, slept in the car, and the next morning I went to this professor's office. I didn't know you had to make an appointment. There I was, camped on his doorstep, along with a hundred hopefuls. His secretary said, 'I don't think he's going to be able to talk to you.' I said, 'I'll wait.' So I waited. I ate lunch there. I read books. He went in and out of his office. Finally, he came out and asked, 'Why are you here?' I said, 'I'm here to see you.'

"I went into his office and somehow, click, click, bang, bang, I managed to catch his attention. That first day in his office he said to me what he says to everybody, 'Your idea sounds great! You're the type who can go out and do it.' And I believed him. I went to a primate habitat and did a project. When I came back, I presented the project to him. He was stunned that I actually did something because most people don't; they just say they want to. And that's how I ended up at the university studying with him. I guess you could say it was all due to luck or being in the right place at the right time or a combination of both."

Today, Carly is a nationally known authority on primates. Like many women, she erroneously ascribes her accomplishments to good fortune rather than to risk-taking and direct action. When we asked the women we interviewed, "What explains why your life has turned out as it has?" most said it was luck or timing. Few women acknowledge their own agency, that is, the power they have used to act on their own behalf. In her history of modern autobiography, *When Memory Speaks*, Jill Ker Conway examines the forces and constraints that prevent women from admitting that ambition, a desire for power, self-confidence, and incredible amounts of effort on their part underlie their professional success. Ker Conway urges women to tell their story in an authoritative voice that shows acceptance of their own agency. She writes, "Could a woman just reverse traditional gender categories, assume the persona of a female Odysseus and set about describing her own heroic life journey? Could even the most rebellious woman throw over the dictates of social conditioning and convince herself, let alone others, that she was her own heroine?" We hope that more women will be able to see that they have already taken the hero's journey and that they have made their own good fortune.

Chapter Five

I Like the Journey
As Much As the Destination

*"There's a divine plan for every soul. As hard as my
lessons have been, they have been equally my blessings. I
needed to do all the things I did to come to where I am now.
We have a great amount of control over our lives and have
a responsibility for who we become. That lesson comes
with age and maturity. We don't always realize when we're
younger that we can create our lives the way we want them
to be."*

Women of this generation did not realize in young adulthood that their individual choices would collectively
reshape the road map for their middle years. Before Torchbearers, the developmental "tasks" for midlife women were
to consolidate, stabilize, resign themselves to life choices, and
settle down. Instead, we found that the women we interviewed
were overcoming detours and obstacles, coping creatively with
traumatic life events, taking risks in love and work, and letting

go of jobs or relationships that no longer met their needs. By weathering major life shifts and learning how to thrive in evolving professional and personal situations, this generation redefined middle age as a time of continued growth and transition. Women of all ages have now come to accept transition and personal change as integral parts of life.

Where are the women of this generation today? In the workplace, they have moved from their first to second, third, or even fourth careers. Despite their ultra-professionalism and the vast amount of time they commit to their jobs, a surprising number of successful women in this age group are in the process of leaving their current careers behind, rather than continuing to do something they fell into or something they chose to do but which now gives them little satisfaction. As one woman who left a high-powered position reports, "I don't need a career to be somebody in the world and to define who I am anymore. I'm not sure what I'll do next, but it will be something that makes a contribution to society." Another states, "I'm still trying to figure out what I'm going to do when I grow up." We have been continually amazed at the chameleon-like ability of women of this generation to transform themselves, their lives, and their circumstances again and again.

On the homefront, they married, divorced, lived with someone new, and remarried. Sue, an accountant and businesswoman, shifted her attention away from the world of work, "Success? I've done that. Right now I'm happy to experience more of a personal life than I've let myself have before." Some went through major upheavals while others coped with losses from traumas such as life-threatening illness and death.

Regardless of what life experiences brought them to the present, all the women we interviewed saw their earlier decisions and choices, both good and bad, as contributing to their current self-knowledge and feeling of authenticity.

Life transitions became the catalyst for personal trans-formation, further self-differentiation, and increased self-esteem. Rather than giving up on life in the face of tragedy, they worked through heartbreak and loss with a renewed sense of courage. Rather than being stuck in a familiar but unsatisfying career or relationship, they made the difficult decision to move on and ride out the storm in order to create a more fulfilling life. Along the way, these women conquered their fears and made the most out of the hands they were dealt. They also regularly took stock of their lives and initiated changes to improve the quality of their lives. As a graphic designer told us, "I finally realized that I needed to decide the parameters I wanted to live the rest of my life by and not be influenced by what happened in the past."

With increased self-confidence that comes with age, they also turned inward to find new arenas for self-knowledge and expression. Why, we wondered, were so many successful women embracing change when they could sit back, revel in their achievements, and simply enjoy the fruits of their labor? The stories in this chapter describe what we learned about how Torchbearers experienced transitional events, became masters of change, and reinvented themselves.

Old Rule: Marry Prince Charming and you'll live happily ever after.

"I felt like a bird in a cage and I wanted to be free."

Although her childhood as the daughter of divorced Asian immigrants was far from typical, Karen expected that her adult life would be a "fairy tale fantasy." She believed that one day she would meet and marry her prince and he would take care of her. Instead, Karen got pregnant her sophomore year in college and felt obligated to marry the baby's father in order to do what was socially acceptable. As a young bride, she had all the trappings of a conventional successful lifestyle: the house, the car, the child, the husband with a good job, and the financial resources to stay home and be a housewife. Still, she found herself wondering, "Is that all there is?" Karen's story is about self-initiated change, tenacity, and the price she paid to leave her fairy tale fantasy behind and gain her hard-won independence.

Like so many women, Karen was raised to live her life for others: "All my actions reflected what would make my husband, my mother, my child, and even my extended family members happy." By the mid-1970s, it seemed the whole world was changing but not her husband. By then she had outgrown the fairytale. "I saw a psychologist for two years and went through a lot of pain trying to decide among three alternatives. One, I could stay in my marriage, play a role, and make everyone's life miserable. Two, I could get a divorce, take my child with me, and repeat the pattern of my mother's life. The last option was to leave my child with my husband, go out on my own, and hope for the best for all of us. I chose the third one. That's when I learned what growing pains were all about."

Karen moved to another city, took a job as a teller at a bank, and eventually secured a branch manager position. She stayed with the same bank for twelve years because she lacked the personal confidence to move to another company or to change professions. A great job offer from a more prestigious bank jolted her into action, but she soon realized that the new position "was just a larger cage." At forty-four, she asked herself, "Why am I doing this?" She was making a lot of money, but she also was under considerable stress. Karen concluded that the job was no longer spiritually right for her, so she bit the bullet and said, "Let's make some changes."

Because she had a strong background in banking and also liked working with older people, Karen became drawn to the idea of assisting the elderly who are no longer able to handle their own finances. As she prepared for a new career as a conservator, she remained solvent by working two part-time jobs as a waitress and a department store clerk—jobs she saw as fun, different, and that she had always wanted to try. She reflects on her experience this way, "I've talked to other people who are doing what they love. There is always a struggle in the beginning. It's important to do what you love. People have talents they never use. If you use your gifts, happiness and money will hopefully come along with it. That's where I'm trying to get to in my life now and I know I'll survive one way or another."

New Truth: Survive and thrive by shaping your destiny.

Karen's life did not move gradually towards some clear goal. It took a quick right turn. At the end of our interview, she told a story which captures the heart of her learning and her disillusion with fairy tale fantasies. "My generation grew up with Snow White and Prince Charming. In *The Paperbag Princess* by Robert

Munsch, a dragon kidnaps a handsome young prince and burns down his castle. The Princess escapes but her dress is badly scorched and all her possessions are destroyed. Still, she sets out to rescue the Prince. She follows the dragon to his lair and knocks on the door. The dragon says, 'Go away. I am preparing a feast—Prince stew.' She says to the dragon, 'I've heard great things about you. They say you're the greatest fire breather ever and can burn a forest down in one breath. Would you show me how you do this?' So the dragon burns down a forest. The Princess says, 'You've burned down one forest, can you burn down seven? Let's see how long it takes you to do that!' The dragon burns down seven forests. Then the Princess says, 'I heard you can fly around the world in nothing flat. Would you show me how you do this?' So the dragon flies around the world. She says, 'Can you fly around the world seven times?' The dragon does that, but when he comes back, he has no fire left.

"The Princess rushes into the dragon's den and frees the Prince who takes one look at her and says, 'Elizabeth, you're a mess. You smell like ashes. Your hair is all tangled. You are wearing a dirty old paper bag. Come back when you are dressed like a real princess.' The Princess replies, 'Your clothes are really pretty. Your hair is very neat. You look like a real prince, but you are a bum. Who needs you!' The Princess goes off into the sunset saying, 'I can survive on my own!' "

Early in her marriage, Karen realized that her childhood expectation of dependence on a man was not what she wanted for herself as an adult. To become her own person, she knew she needed to learn self-reliance. Before making her decision to leave, Karen carefully examined all options and consequences.

With help, she found the courage to make the difficult choice to live separately from her child in order to gain her independence. While many women believe they just "fell into things," most, like Karen, prepared for opportunities and then positioned themselves to be in the right place at the right time. Realizing they could be active agents in their own lives, they followed their hearts even when there was a big price to pay. Karen not only learned that she could survive on her own, but she also learned to thrive in a competitive work environment. Now in mid-life, she has chosen once again to leave the safe and familiar by continuing her commitment to do work she loves and to operate her own business.

Old Rule: Be grateful for what you have.

> *"It was very empowering when I made the shift from being a peripheral counterculture person to an owner of a successful business."*

Unlike Karen, Laura's future was not purposefully planned and her career directions evolved circumstantially. Taking advantage of the times and having the flexibility to pursue her interest in women's issues, Laura initially changed life directions simply because she wanted to. What she lacked in skills, she made up for in risk-taking. In contrast to the traditional model of work in which people hold a single job in one place for their entire life, women like Laura paved the way for viewing career shifts and personal change as an ongoing, natural part of life.

In her twenties, Laura married a wealthy older man. Freed from economic worries, she organized demonstrations, joined a consciousness raising group, and lobbied for women's quality-of-life issues. From these experiences, Laura realized there was no turning back to a pre-feminist position. "Once you understand the issue of equal rights for women and people of color and see the world in socio-economic terms, then you see inequality everywhere," she says. "Figuring out how to position yourself in society once you've made a shift in consciousness and have a new vision is difficult." At the same time, her husband wanted an open marriage, which Laura found totally unacceptable. She began her personal search by divorcing her husband and moving from the East to the West Coast.

Laura remembers the early '80s as the hardest time in her life. As a divorced single woman, she helped raise five children belonging to members of the collective with whom she lived. Laura shared her hefty divorce settlement with the collective, leaving herself with no money in the end. For all of her maturity and life experience, she had very little practice in money management and didn't know how to protect herself financially.

After years of doing self-help counseling, Laura, now broke, chose to become a "barefoot therapist—a hairdresser" at a time when issues of beauty and image were becoming divisive not only in the women's movement, but within the Left as well. She remembers "the intolerance of some in the women's movement who would question a person's feminism if she wore lipstick or shaved her legs. When I decided to become a hairdresser, it was a downwardly mobile move, even though many of my friends saw it as a politically correct choice." Ignoring her critics, Laura continued her political work on women's issues, finished beauty school, and opened her own hair salon. "As a feminist, success had to do with the quality of what I had created, not with how much money I made. I realized I was very creative in terms of my talent with hair and I had a flair for working with people."

When the '80s economy took a downturn, many small business owners felt the pinch. Laura also experienced the pressure to keep her business afloat. She turned to drugs and alcohol as an escape. "At that point, we were all fairly arrogant about how immune we were to such things becoming a problem," says Laura. "Cocaine was not addictive and we had it under control, or so we thought. But we didn't have it under control. We blew a lot of money and I believe it gave us a false sense of community."

After two years, Laura realized she had a drug and alcohol problem. "I was in a series of pathetic relationships," she admits. "I managed to maintain a strong public persona, but I could feel the hypocrisy. Something had to change. Finally I hit bottom and reached for help. It's been ten years since I stopped drinking, abusing drugs, and smoking. I got help and started the process of coming back to myself. At the time, the recovery community was full of young people like myself who were dually dependent. We had ridiculed our parents for burying themselves in a bottle of scotch and valium, yet we were doing the same thing with good wine and cocaine."

New Truth: Keep reaching for the brass ring.

Throughout her addiction and recovery, Laura managed not only to hold on to her business, but to shape it in some new directions. When Laura decided to expand her salon, she established an art gallery where she showcased handcrafted jewelry and sculpture by local artists. "In the course of an hour in an art-filled, comfortable, holistic environment, I could sculpt an image that made my clientele feel really good about themselves."

After receiving the award for "Best Salon" in her geographic area for several years in a row, Laura was ready to move on, even though she wasn't sure what the outcome would be. First, she turned to her primary relationship of five years, faced the disappointing realization that it would never be emotionally supportive enough to sustain having children, and ended it. Then she went to Greece and fell deeply in love with a man whom she later discovered was married, a circumstance she couldn't reconcile with being a feminist. She returned home, vowing to no longer suffer because of a man's immaturity, "I felt like it was always bootcamp and training—showing up, being present, giving it my best shot, only to find that it wasn't enough." Within the next year she sold her business, began to create her own art, and became romantically involved with a woman. "As I turned forty, I felt the pressure of my biological clock, the accumulated disappointments with men, and the fortification of my politics as a feminist. Right now, I'd say I am leaping into the 21st century. I just wish I had more of a long-term sense of what I want and how to get it, but I wasn't trained in any of that," she concludes.

Women like Laura are trailblazing new patterns of self-fulfillment in their middle years by choosing to change the shape and quality of their lives. They are adding or subtracting partners, building families, starting new careers, and pursuing intuitive directions for personal growth. Laura sold her salon and moved to a rural area with her partner. She used her artistic talents to launch a new business designing greeting cards with her own photographs. After several unsuccessful attempts to become pregnant through in vitro fertilization, Laura and her partner recently adopted a baby girl. More mature and self-confident, she anticipates reinventing herself as a mother for the next period of her life. Having come a long way from being the young wife of an older man, Laura acknowledges her business accomplishments, recognizes her creativity, and feels "happy to be alive." While still uncertain about what the future will hold, she knows she can count on her instincts and entrepreneurial spirit to see her through.

Old Rule: Don't make waves.

> "I began to realize how much I intellectualized my life and had put everything in compartments. One day, I suddenly began to feel like an orchestra inside, but I knew I had a lot more tuning up to do to be ready for the concert."

Marianne, the daughter of a cantor, grew up in a state of blissful innocence with powerful parental expectations of her becoming a traditional Jewish wife and mother. Although she chose to major in mathematics, a nontraditional field for women, she never imagined at the time that her life would represent such a radical departure from her family's values. Marianne initially followed the program by marrying a Jewish man, but then broke family tradition by moving three thousand miles away after a cross-country motorcycle trip to California. In mid-life, she divorced her husband and, against her parents' wishes, married a man from a very different religious background. "I would have never in a million years dreamed that I would do such a thing."

After making this dramatic life change, she experienced several planned and unplanned transitions that radically affected other aspects of her existence. Her story illustrates how self-initiated change and unanticipated life events can contribute to creating a climate for expanding our capabilities well beyond parental parameters.

"I was seven months pregnant when my husband Jack's brain exploded, nearly killing him. There were no symptoms. Boom! He had a terrible headache, started throwing up, and couldn't see. I rushed him to the hospital and they put him right into intensive care." Her husband had suffered a potentially life-threatening aneurysm. She remembers screaming to herself in the car that night, "What am I going to do now? What if Jack doesn't live?" Miraculously, Jack's surgery was successful and he remained in the hospital for a week. The first night he returned home, they went to their first Lamaze class and shortly thereafter, their daughter was born. "The biggest thing I learned during this period was how totally unpredictable everything is and how completely out-of-control life can be."

After her baby was born, Marianne shared a teaching position with a colleague. She felt pride in her work, and while her job as a teacher enabled her to use her skills and creativity, it was also very demanding and stressful. She was approaching burnout, so she enrolled in cake-decorating classes in order to relax. "I found it interesting and I was good at it. I always loved to bake but I never thought I'd do anything with it professionally until somebody said, 'You should do this as a business.' I thought about it for a few seconds and surprised myself by saying, 'Why not?'"

New Truth: Ride the wave of change.

With the family crisis over, a secure job, and more free time available now that the baby was older, Marianne realized she was in an optimal position to start something new. "I'm the kind of person who does things slowly," she says. "I don't jump right into things. First, I got business cards. Then, I made my first cake for a friend's fortieth birthday party. After that, I realized I had to have pictures of cakes to show people what I could do. I bought some Styrofoam cake forms, decorated each one differently, and photographed them on a table in the back yard. Then, I wiped off the icing and did more decorative designs. I created eight or ten 'cakes,' had the pictures blown up, and put them in a portfolio. I would tell prospective clients that these were actual wedding or birthday cakes. I did the designs, so I didn't feel like a total fraud. It was the only way I could think of to get started. I couldn't just say, 'Take my word for it.' I advertised and started getting some jobs. Then, it was word of mouth and more advertising. All of a sudden, I had a business. Me, a business person? I didn't even belong to the Chamber of Commerce! It's funny, but now even *I* define myself as an entrepreneur.

"The hardest thing about my transition was going from what I consider a noble profession like teaching to baking cakes and having that be OK. I had to figure out a way to justify it to myself. It wasn't good enough to just say I want to do something different with my life. If I had become a social worker or a doctor or some other respected professional, that would have been easier. Finally I had to ask myself, 'What did I do with my students when I was teaching? I helped them to learn more than how to survive and be productive members of society. I taught them the importance of enjoying their lives and being happy.' Sometimes I think that what I do now is not a big deal, but other times I see it as very creative work. I'm doing something that makes other people happy, but most of all, I feel fulfilled as well."

Beginning with her divorce, Marianne found the courage to keep going even when the earth shifted beneath her feet. She weathered the life-threatening illness of her second husband during her first pregnancy and gave birth to her daughter—two major life events in close proximity. Her decision to change careers, however, was motivated by a desire to do something different with her life. Like so many women of this generation who fell into their first careers or who followed the advice of parents or mentors, she chose to make what Betty Morris in a *Fortune* magazine article called a "major mid-life course correction." Marianne left a secure position in education to become an entrepreneur. Having initiated and completed the transition, she now encourages other women to break free from external standards and do what makes them happy. And yes, Marianne even joined the Chamber of Commerce. When she looks back on her choices, however, she values most her mother's words, offered several years after her remarriage, "I really admire you for doing what you want with your life."

Old Rule: Give up your power when you marry.

> *"Everything that's ever happened to me has pushed me to another level. Right now my life is condensing like a sauce that's being reduced down to the essence. At the bottom of the pot is going to be that gem, that thing that we all search*

for. I like the journey more than the destination. The act of trying to get there has always been more important to me than arriving."

Middle age brought not only the good elements of life to Torchbearers, but also their biggest life challenges. Sometimes the most significant events of life are unplanned and unwanted. In such circumstances, many of the women we interviewed, driven by the sheer enormity of the task of surviving, were forced to rely on past coping strategies. When all was said and done, they had also cultivated new inner and outer resources which enabled them to grow beyond their current state of affairs. From the tragic loss of her child, Gerry emerged a stronger, wiser person who became more committed than ever to her artistic career and to honoring her daughter's spirit.

Gerry became pregnant after three years of what she believed to be a happy marriage. The walls came tumbling down when she had to have a cesarean delivery. Her husband, unable to handle the situation, left Gerry at the hospital and went to a bar where he picked up a woman and spent the night with her. She found out from their roommate and confronted her husband. "He told me the truth, but it was really downhill from there because I learned later that he was sleeping with a lot of women. He also gave me gonorrhea when I was pregnant and I had to have massive doses of penicillin," she says.

Additional strain on the already shaky marriage followed when her new baby daughter began having epileptic seizures. Gerry, however, somehow kept it together because it was important for her to preserve the illusion of their family being intact.

But the marriage crumbled beyond repair after the young couple experienced a terrible tragedy, the accidental drowning of their three-year-old daughter. "At that point, there was just no staying together anymore. To be with someone I was already feeling ambivalent about in a situation where we shared this tremendous loss was too much. It was one more nail in the coffin." After many unsuccessful attempts to make things work by subsuming her needs to those of her husband, Gerry decided to leave the marriage and try to get on with her life.

New Truth: Use your power to heal.

Gerry always catered more to others' needs than her own. After her daughter's death, she was able to turn that life pattern around. "My daughter's gift to me was my own consciousness," Gerry says. "I had to look at myself and say, 'You've been doing things for other people for a long time. When are you going to start doing things for yourself?' I had no one. My father and daughter died the same year I divorced my husband. I literally woke up one morning with nothing and I had to reconstruct from there."

Gerry stayed with her sister and mother after her daughter's death. Almost catatonic, she could neither talk nor eat. The loss of her child felt like "someone was ripping my arms and legs off. I had no access to myself. I was a hollow woman. Everything had emptied itself out. The greatest challenge for me was, at age thirty-nine, to answer the question: How do I fill it up again? Needless to say, it took a long time to heal.

"One night I went to bed asking for a sign that would give me the impetus to go on. I don't know if I was hallucinating, but someone spoke to me. It was very dream-like. The room seemed to fill up with red smoke. I could smell it. I looked up and saw myself in the sky. I was a bird covered with bright colored feathers, diving into a body of water at a very fast speed. I felt myself go under the warm water. Then a large hand pulled me up by the back of my neck and put me on a barge where there was a chair. Someone put a crown on my head and started floating me down the river. The mist was enveloping me and I heard someone telling me that I had power, that I was going to survive and heal, and that I was going to use my power."

The next morning Gerry awoke with an appetite. She got a job, went back to school, and earned a master's degree in fine arts. "From that point on, I felt I had taken control of myself in a way that I had never done before." Perhaps because of her own troubled childhood, Gerry had stayed in a bad marriage and tenaciously worked to build a family. In spite of disappointments, she was able to pick up the pieces and create a new beginning in mid-life. Eventually, she established an art studio and remarried. Building on her insights and deepened sense of self-worth, Gerry constructed a peaceful haven for productive work.

Old Rule: Marry a man your own age.

"If I had to write a description of what I thought my knight in shining armor on a white horse would look like, he wouldn't be seventeen years older than I am, have two kids, a couple of ex-wives, and not want any more children."

Diane's parents held high expectations for their children, encouraging risk-taking within conventional boundaries and praising profusely for good behavior. As a result, Diane felt she grew into adulthood with a high need for other's validation. She was a successful, career-oriented college administrator in her thirties when she met and fell in love with Dave, a colleague seventeen years her senior. When Diane followed her heart and married him, she faced strong parental disapproval, problematic relations with his two grown children, and the improbability of having children of her own. She also left a position in which she had amassed many accomplishments and had defined herself professionally. By going through this period of high stress and acting against her family's wishes, Diane not only became her own person, but also developed solid coping resources that she would soon need again.

After they relocated from Oregon to Massachusetts and reconciled with his children, Diane and Dave finally settled down to build a new life together. Diane chose a new career direction and enrolled in graduate school. With a new position for Dave, they quickly made friends, became involved in the community, and bought a house. Then, a series of unexpected health problems impacted their life. Some people who experience unanticipated life challenges, such as loss of a loved one or illness, come to see themselves as victims. Diane, however, rolled with the punches and took things in stride.

In a two-year period, Dave had one major health crisis and Diane had two. Dave's illness, originally misdiagnosed as a middle-ear infection, turned out to be a stroke. "When we got the news, we were both scared, but other people said we responded very calmly and matter-of-factly. We didn't seem overly distraught because it's our style to handle challenges in an appearingly easy way. If we had found out the day after he had his stroke, we might have lived and acted very differently than finding out six weeks later. Fortunately, even though he probably had several more mini-strokes, Dave went back to work within a week."

Shortly thereafter, Diane developed a painful back and neck problem. Finished with her master's degree and working in a different career, Diane had just begun doctoral studies. Her program was very challenging and required major lifestyle changes. She recalls, "Maybe I was stressed in a way that I didn't know and it went to my weakest point, which was my neck. I've always wondered whether that was just my way of taking care of myself. I dropped out of life for two months, took care of my back, and thought about whether I really wanted to continue in school." Several doctors wanted to perform a high-risk surgical procedure. One part of Diane wanted to do what she was told, but the other doubted whether the surgery was necessary. She decided not to have the surgery and, within a few months, her condition improved.

Within a year of recovering from the back problem, Diane was diagnosed with a kidney tumor. Her doctor was sure it was not malignant, but Diane felt less certain because the statistics were against her. "I never was nervous about having surgery, but I was scared about what the results were going to be. I've learned that you can't control everything. You think that your life is going along and you are in control. You make your plans, develop your interests, get a job, enroll in school, and then you get sick. Getting sick changes things. This wasn't what I thought life was going to be like. Was I doing what I really wanted to do?

While these are typical mid-life crisis questions, it seemed premature for me to be asking them at age thirty-eight."

As she did with Dave's illness, Diane responded in a calm, logical way. "My friends and family were more upset than I was. I wonder whether people who are in the midst of illnesses handle it more easily than those around them do. That's why I wasn't as frightened as I could or should have been. I just say, 'OK, this is what I have in front of me.' "

New Truth: When you marry for "better," you can handle the "worse."

While the life transitions Diane experienced could have thrown her off course, they simply became part of the flotsam and jetsam of her life. "There have been turning points in my life that might seem really big, but I would just say to myself, 'I see what needs to be done, so I'm just going to do it.' As a result of both our illnesses, Dave and I have spent a lot of time asking ourselves whether we want our lives to be so stressful. Is our work that important to us? How can we make significant changes? Can we give up what we're doing? How do we get more balance in life and what does that look like? I'm fairly young to be thinking about these kinds of issues. Maybe if I were ten years older I'd feel comfortable not striving for success, but up until now that has been an important part of who I am. It would not be OK to just drop out."

Recently, Dave had major, life-threatening surgery. Temporarily shaken yet again by the possibility of losing the man she loves, Diane took a break from school and relied on the skills she honed through coping with their previous illnesses. When her husband recovered and returned to work, Diane resumed her doctoral studies. By facing in her late thirties what most people don't have to deal with until much later in life, Diane gained a deeper appreciation of what really matters. Their marriage became more solid as a result of the couple supporting each other through their separate illnesses. In addition, Diane and Dave enjoyed three long trips so that they could spend time together in good health. Throughout this difficult period of her life, Diane continued to pursue her career goals, but at a slower pace. More importantly, she learned how to adapt, modify, and re-evaluate her priorities to achieve a more balanced life.

Old Rule: Accept what you can't change.

"Life isn't a straight line."

Lisa, like Diane, chose to re-order her priorities in mid-life when faced with her father's terminal illness. Her story, however, is about generosity and making the world a better place for others, even when she could not directly benefit from the effort. Lisa gave little thought to her own needs during her years of involvement in the anti-war, feminist, and labor movements. Her parents never understood why their only child would choose to organize workers in Central America during the middle of a war. She recalls, "If they really knew what was going on, they would have been even more worried." When her dad became terminally ill, Lisa returned home to be with him and help her mother. The time spent with her parents became a turning point in her life. By watching her mother care for her father, she gained a different perspective on marriage. "In the past, I always felt there would be time for home and family in the future. There was always time. At age thirty-three, I suddenly realized that maybe I was running out of time," she says. After her father died, she decided to remain in Chicago rather than return to her work in Central America.

"That night," Lisa says, "I went out to a rally to protest government policies in El Salvador and met my husband. We have been together ever since. In the years when I was sexually liberated, I used the Dalkon shield, never knowing that a third of the women who did became sterile. When I tried to conceive, I suffered three ectopic pregnancies, one of which nearly killed me. Finally, I realized I wasn't going to have children in the usual way. I had medical insurance so I decided to try in vitro fertilization. The HMO kept stalling on whether to authorize the procedure. Eventually, they told me I couldn't have it because it was no longer part of my health care plan. I sued them for refusing to approve the procedure. I was able to prove that they had waited to make a decision until coverage was excluded from my policy. I found a lawyer with infertility problems herself who constructed a class action suit and we won." Unfortunately, when Lisa finally was able to have in vitro fertilization covered by her insurance, it didn't work. The outcome of the lawsuit, however, subsequently affected over five thousand women who had also been denied the opportunity to have the procedure.

New Truth: Change what you can't accept.

Now forty years old, Lisa decided to stop trying to get pregnant and began to channel her energy into broader issues affecting women and children. "Since I couldn't have children of my own,

I decided to pursue some pseudo-mother-type activities. The first thing I did was to start a child-care center at the hospital where I worked. After starting child-care centers and working in them in Central America, I thought, 'Why can't I do that here?' I was very active in the health professionals' union at the hospital and vowed to convince the leadership that women employees needed to have a place at work for their children."

A long struggle followed. Lisa spent over two years fighting the hospital administration tooth and nail. Finally, the center was approved, funds were allocated, and contracts were offered. One day, while they were celebrating over a glass of wine, a co-worker told Lisa that she had given birth to a daughter because of a class action lawsuit. Unaware that it was Lisa's lawsuit, her colleague said, "My husband and I had traveled to Europe to celebrate or cry about the fact that I was forty-three and didn't have children. I resolved my feelings of disappointment, returned home, and found a letter in the mail saying that I was being offered in vitro fertilization as a result of a suit which had been won. I gave it a try and my daughter was conceived." In retelling her co-worker's story, Lisa reflected, "I tried in vitro but I never got pregnant. Still, the struggle made it possible for somebody else to have a child. What I did definitely affected somebody's life and that was really important for me to hear."

Over the last seven years, Lisa has become deeply involved in horticulture and plant propagation. She now tends several hundred fruit trees. "For me, working in a garden has become my source of spirituality—what I consider must be what other people get out of feeling some kind of contact with something that might last beyond the time they die. That's the only way I can conceivably relate to any of it. I take classes and meet people who are interested in plants, native plant preservation, environmental protection, and nature experiences. Plus, I love it." Although not what she originally intended, Lisa found a fulfilling way to meet her need to nurture life and growth.

The journey continues

Torchbearers anticipate continued change in their lives. We asked the women we interviewed what they see as the central issues in their lives right now. They identified spirituality, career, health and aging, money, elderly parents, political activism, marriage, family and children, and friendships. By far, though, the most common theme was spirituality.

> "As Nature takes away our physical capabilities, she gives
> us this wonderful thing, this wisdom and maturity."

Most of the women we interviewed say their present lives are not about conforming to traditional notions of success—money, power, or fame that are visible to others. As Leslie, owner of an accounting firm, told us, "The last ten years have been about proving to myself that I had the ability, strength, and stamina to do whatever I set my mind to do. As my father's daughter, I learned to compete in the world, to do business, and to keep twenty-five balls in the air at once. While this certainly has empowered me, I feel the deeper issues of my femininity and my spirituality need time and expression. By going inward, I know I'll find different outward expressions."

Definitions of spirituality varied, but the most commonly mentioned include a sense of well-being and integration. "It doesn't matter how much money you have and how good your career is," one woman told us. "If you don't feel good about your life, it's all the same. Spirituality is about a perspective on life and an understanding of how all the parts go together. It's an understanding about how your thoughts create your own life and experiences." Thus, spirituality for many women of this generation has little to do with traditional religious experience.

A successful real estate broker, who recently has begun to meditate regularly, views spiritual growth as the experience of the simple gifts of life, "I'm stopping to smell the roses and maybe now I'd like to have a garden."

Judy, a marketing director and massage therapist, told us, "Spirituality is a core issue that impacts all other questions about everything else." Five years ago her interest in ancient religious practices led her into Shamanic ritual and healing rites in aboriginal cultures. "It triggered something very primal and instinctual for me, addressing a void that I had been seeking to fill for myself. I did so very cautiously because I was afraid of destroying the spiritual foundations I had already built and I wasn't sure how everything would merge and become whole. What's important right now is integrating the natural me that's very earthy, very connected to bodily functions, very connected to cycles with rhythms, music, drumming, art, sound, and healing. How can I possibly integrate that with my current lifestyle as a corporate executive? I'm having a hell of a time. I have a lot more questions than answers." Since our interview, Judy quit her job and relocated to another state. Recently, she sent us an announcement for a workshop at her newly created center for women's spirituality.

"I'm going to like being old."

The women we interviewed express a healthy perspective on the aging process, often pointing to the positive aspects of growing older that can balance out the less desirable features. Annie, a human resource specialist, reports a change in the focus of her attention, "I work at my profession, but my emphasis has shifted away from that now because I'm established. I'm on cruise control. The most important things in life are health, happiness, friends, and my relationship. Right now, I'm also having to look at the aging issue. I'm seeing the face and body starting to go, so I've started working out for the first time in my life." Annie will have plenty of company. Fitness and body image are central issues for women in their late forties. Most of the interviewees express their desire to take care of themselves so they can continue to look attractive, resolve ongoing weight issues, and/or maintain their vitality.

Concerns about health, illness, and the medical system occupy the minds of others. Claire, who unexpectedly lost a dear friend to cancer, expressed her fears, "I find myself worrying about something that hasn't happened yet, but if it did, I'd know how to deal with it, just as my friend did. But I don't like *worrying* about getting old and what the next thirty years are going to be like. I never worried about these things before. I've made major decisions without thinking about the future, never contributed to a retirement account, or even thought about it, for that matter. Now I am. On the other hand, I also think, 'Retirement? God, I could die tomorrow. Why am I saving for retirement?' " For the most part, though, the women we interviewed view their aging process as a natural part of life and talk about what they need to do now so that their later years will be happy and satisfying.

A central issue for Torchbearers is caring for aging parents. Without exception, all the women who identified this as an issue intend to become more involved in the lives of their elderly parents or already are actively participating. One woman softly cried as she recounted fulfilling her father's lifelong dream to visit Yellowstone National Park, "The first time he saw the geysers he started to cry, he was so moved! The fact that I could give something back to him like that was really fantastic for me." When and where to move a parent who can no longer live independently concerns several women, as well as sibling problems, financial concerns, and mixed feelings about accepting responsibility for a parent. Marge poignantly summed up her situation, "Dealing with my sick mother is an issue of time and an issue of emotion. It's sobering to realize that she is at the end of her life and that she will never be the mother I wanted her to be." Letting go of childhood resentments and accepting parents' limitations have enabled many women to move forward with their lives.

The search continues

> "I'm not afraid to do something that's never been done before. The older I get, the more confident I am."

Having smoothed out the rough edges in young adulthood, many women realize they have more control over their lives than they think and can actively shape their own futures. As one woman says, "I feel like time is getting shorter. If you're still not doing what you really feel you need to be doing with your life, you have to keep pushing, make changes, and let things go. You can't be stuck." For other women, the issue of creating a balance between work and other aspects of their lives occupies their thoughts. Ann Marie, who owns her own business, told us, "I need to find out what balance is and take steps to achieve it. I need more time to experiment and be creative again, to play. I haven't taken any vacations. I've spent years working seven days a week, ten hours a day until the point where I burned myself out. I find I'm rebelling against things that I need to do because the little girl part of me just doesn't want to do them anymore!"

As a generation, baby boomers are still striving to improve the quality of their lives and the lives of others. As Barbara, a school administrator told us, "I have a moderate degree of success, I'm making decent money, I have a wonderful child and a strong marriage, but it's not enough. I'm looking for something to fill the gaps." If there are lessons to be learned from these women in mid-life, they could be summed up as: 1) Go forward, even if you are afraid; 2) Trust your instincts; 3) Embrace change; and 4) Take risks to get what you want. Having let go of self-limitations and the "baggage" of early adulthood, the women of this generation are now acting from a stronger, inner-directed perspective that reflects the integration of their experiences and values. Whether the "gaps" will be filled by self-exploration, community betterment activities, more rewarding work, or more fulfilling relationships, this generation of women can be counted on to pursue their dreams well into old age.

Part Two

Who We Are As A Generation

Chapter Six

I've Made Lifestyle Choices
That Surprised Even Me

"My mother's position on family life never wavered. It is intractable. To this day I receive phone calls whose opening lines a writer could spend months inventing. Two of these have become legend: 1) 'Your sister-in-law is pregnant and that means more to me than a million dollars or any play,' and 2) 'Now that there's a writer's strike, maybe you should think about law school.' The latter may seem mild but it happened to arrive on the same day that I learned I had won a $10,000 playwriting grant."

—Wendy Wasserstein, playwright

"Have sown my wild oats. Ready now for marriage and family."

—Torchbearer's personal ad

Not so long ago, having a daughter who was "an old maid," "knocked up," or "living in sin" was a family's private shame. But beginning in the late 1960s, hundreds of thousands of nice, middle-class, young women began to experiment with what were considered to be scandalous behaviors. Torchbearers not only created powerful new strategies for succeeding in the world of work, but they have also been instrumental in pioneering a wide variety of lifestyle choices for women. While there have always been some women in each era willing to break from convention, this generation was the first to make the large-scale adoption of previously unacceptable conduct both commonplace and sanctioned by the larger society. It would not be an exaggeration to say that they are responsible for transforming the way "nice girls" of all ages now choose to lead their lives.

The transition from prim, rule-bound, dutiful daughters into brash and daring not-so-good young women seemed to happen overnight. Sheila remembers her own metamorphosis, "The change came so quickly. I was sickeningly perfect in high school. I thought it was wrong to pet heavily, even if you were engaged! Within a matter of months, I threw everything I thought was written in stone out the window." Torchbearers may have paused momentarily before jumping into bed with a handsome stranger or getting birth control for the first time, but they didn't hesitate for long. As one woman told us, "There was a window of opportunity between the pill and herpes when a lot of sexual action could happen without hardly any consequences, except emotional ones, and we weren't really thinking about those." In the 1970s and 1980s, they became the first in their family to live openly with a lover, give birth to a child as a single parent, get divorced, or marry someone from a different race or religion. Not too long ago, such actions were viewed as shocking and even shameful.

Essayist Barbara Ehrenrich writes, "If either sex has gone through a change in sexual attitudes and behavior that deserves to be called revolutionary, it is women, and not men at all. This fact should be widely known because it leaps out from all the polls and surveys that count for data in these matters. Put briefly, men have changed their sexual behavior very little in the decades from the '50s to the '80s. They 'fooled around,' got married, and often fooled around some more, much as their fathers and perhaps their grandfathers had before them. Women, however, have gone from a pattern of virginity before marriage and monogamy thereafter to a pattern that much more resembles men's."

In the course of a typical Torchbearer's lifetime there has been a dramatic shift in the rules for female sexual and social conduct. When author Cheryl Merser compares the behavior of her generation to her mother's, she concludes, "[We] might as well have come from different centuries or different planets." Fran, forty-four, views her own experience as a prime example of the experiential chasm between generations, "My mother and her peers didn't get divorced. They didn't have dependable birth control or readily available safe and legal abortion. They didn't have careers. They were homemakers. My life would be very different if I didn't have the choices I had when I was eighteen."

Girls who grew up in the 1950s and early 1960s had a picture of a certain kind of lifestyle they would have by the time they were adults. The reality is quite different from what they had envisioned.

Old Rule: Go to college, get married, have kids.

"I grew up believing that the normal adult woman married early and had children automatically."

Women today are having babies at older ages, often while unmarried. They are delaying marriage or foregoing it altogether, divorcing and heading single-parent families, and spending a greater portion of their lives without the companionship and economic support of a male partner. Torchbearers were the first generation of women able to choose among work, motherhood, or both. Their choices have been influenced by several concerns: 1) Would they be able to find a partner to build a stable relationship with who also shared an interest in having children? An additional complication exists because marriage no longer holds the promise of permanence nor does the presence of children guarantee male economic support. 2) With the responsibilities of marriage and/or children, could they still take full advantage of demanding professional obligations? 3) Given the lack of social support for both full-time mothers and high-level career women, how do they make choices without subjecting themselves to disapproval that undermines whatever decision they make?

Of those we interviewed, the majority were either previously married or had lived with a partner at least once. Less than 5 percent had neither cohabited nor married, yet, *only 19 percent are currently in their first marriage.* Given that a sizable number married for the first time after thirty-five, there is a surprisingly low success rate for marriages that began when they were young.

There used to be four marital status categories: single, married, divorced, and widowed. In a "traditional" relationship, a woman usually marries and remains married to her original spouse. In our sample, we identified thirty other types of relationship patterns that they are currently involved in. Trying to unravel all the possible combinations of previous relationships from the marital history data has been both confusing and amusing. These new categories include "divorced once, never cohabited;" "divorced twice, cohabited once;" "cohabited once, never married;" etc. Each of these categories contains several patterns; for example, under "divorced once, cohabited once" (DOCO), there are DOCO women who are now single, as well as those who have remarried, and those who are now cohabiting but not married. Consider these combinations: "divorced once, cohabited once, lesbian now;" "divorced twice, cohabited four times, single now;" "two previous lesbian relationships, married now." Understandable is the joke about the man in his forties who only dates very young women. When asked why, he replies, "Their stories are shorter."

New Truth: If you can't replicate the past, assemble something new.

"I've come to terms with the fact that a lot of things didn't turn out the way I expected."

Susan is forty-three, single, and childless, a situation she never expected for herself but one she has come to terms with. "Women of our mother's generation had desires," she says, "but they couldn't give in to them the way we did. Our mothers didn't have options. I hope the next generation won't have to make an either/or choice—home and kids or a career. When I see a woman who has an admirable career and children, I'm in awe. I will always feel there's something slightly defective about me because I couldn't do both. I have little patience for women my age who are whining now about not having children when every step of the way, every bit of birth control they used, every guy they picked, every job they took, and every abortion they had, they made a decision not to marry or have a child."

The generation of women who led the baby boom basically felt eternally young and hopeful. The realities of some of the decisions made along the way, however, caught up with them as they entered middle age. The abortion that they were so relieved about, the marriage proposal they turned down, the decision to live with a man who was not a promising life partner ("But I love him," she told everyone.) were choices made in the past; there might be some regret now, but that goes along with being a trailblazer.

Jane is both a successful attorney and an artist. Once swept away by the dazzling array of professional and interpersonal alternatives opening to women, she freely admits that, due to an absence of role models, her decisions were often made by default. She had a twelve-year cohabiting relationship that began in her early twenties. It was a difficult and stressful relationship which she wanted to leave but didn't because her partner had serious health problems. Today she is forty-one, single, and grappling with yet another concern.

"I live alone," Jane told us. "Finding a mate is my big issue because I'm reaching an age where I have to resolve the children question. I have several friends who are single mothers by

choice. I have one single girlfriend who was artificially insemi-
nated so I'm aware of the options but I'm very conflicted about
whether to do that. Recently, I became seriously ill myself for
the first time. It scared me and made me realize how hard it is to
be alone. You feel vulnerable and get a glimpse of what might
happen at an older age. I find this issue about having children,
whether I'm in a relationship or not, still unresolved." Jane now
realizes that the choices she made, or didn't make, had consequences down the road. Her ultimate decision about marriage
and children may appear to be made by default, but in fact, Jane
can select from an array of alternatives not available to previous
generations of women. She can choose any pattern for herself—
marry, stay single, have children, adopt—all without fear of family or societal approbation. And, of course, she may just choose
to do nothing.

Old Rule: Wait for the Prince.

> *"I don't much like to think that being a bachelor girl limits
> how you see the world. On the other hand, I know it cer-
> tainly limits how the world sees you."*
> **—Wendy Wasserstein, playwright**

Many Torchbearers grew up believing that someday their prince
would come. Diane has deeply traditional values and aspirations,
yet she has never married. "When I turned thirty, I said, 'I
haven't met a man yet that I want to marry. Now it's going to
happen.' It was always just going to happen. I was raised to
believe that you went to college, met a man, got married, and

had kids. We were expected to do everything our mothers did, except now we were also going to have careers. Although getting married right away wasn't my focus, here I am—forty-three and single."

Several years ago, Diane tried a unique group therapy. The therapist brought men and women together to date over a two-month period. She went out with each of the men twice. At the therapy sessions, they would talk about how their dates went. She says, "My reasons for going were to feel more comfortable about saying how I really feel and to learn how to deliver criticism and not feel horrible about it or without the other person feeling damaged. As the therapist said, the real test will be when I meet somebody I'm romantically attracted to." Diane still hopes to be in a long-term relationship. If she met somebody this year and he seemed like the right person, she would try to have a child. She acknowledges that she never thought she'd be facing this decision in her forties. She says, "I assumed that someday Prince Charming would knock on my door, just like that."

New Truth: If the Prince doesn't show up, go door to door.

> "The first night we met, he asked 'How come you're not married?' I was only twenty-four but I had been asked this question so often I had an answer ready. 'My husband died in a car accident.' "
>
> **—Sara Davidson, author**

Based on a 1986 study conducted at Yale University, an inaccurate report specified that college-educated women of a certain age were going to have a hard time getting married. According to these researchers, never-married thirty-year-old college graduates had only a 20 percent chance of marrying; by thirty-five, the odds were 5 percent; by forty, the odds were less than 2 percent. College-educated African-American women had even lower odds. If men marry younger women, then women born between 1945 and 1955 would have to marry older men who represented a smaller group since the baby-boom population was much larger than previous generations. Eventually, a researcher from the U.S. Census Bureau for Marriage and Family Statistics refuted this report and concluded that, at thirty, the never-married, college-educated woman had a 58 percent to 66 percent chance of marriage (three times the Yale prediction); at thirty-five, the odds were 32 percent to 41 percent (seven times higher); at forty, the odds were 17 percent to 23 percent (twenty-three times higher). Not surprisingly, these revised figures received far less media attention than the original report.

Many women have beaten the odds by marrying or starting a family in their late thirties or forties. Julie, a self-employed business consultant married for the first time at age forty-one. Although she was very proud of her career, Julie felt dissatisfied with her personal relationships. It wasn't until she made a job out of finding a husband that her future mate came into her life. "I was reading books on how to meet men, what to do, where to go, and I was doing and going but I wasn't meeting the right guy," Julie admits. "One day, on the Oprah Winfrey show, I saw a woman who had written a book about applying the basics of advertising to finding a man. Advertisers don't employ just one method. They use posters, displays, TV ads, cold calling, marketing, etc. That made a lot of sense, so I acquiesced, joined a dating service, and started answering and placing personal ads. I dated like crazy with the purpose of finding a husband."

Julie also placed a personal ad saying she was a fun-loving, vivacious red head. As a result, she met a lot of red-head-loving fun guys. Then, one day a friend called and said, 'If you really want to meet a man, your next ad should say: 'Have sown my wild oats. Ready now for marriage and family.'' " That was the ad that attracted the man who became her husband. One year after her marriage, Julie, at age forty-two, gave birth to a son.

Like Julie, Cindy waited a long time to marry. There was a recent period in her life when she intentionally chose to have nothing to do with men. This was sparked by her grief over the death of her father. Cindy is an only child; her mother had passed away several years earlier. Fearful that she would bring too much excess baggage into future relationships, she recognized that she needed time for herself. As a result, Cindy stopped dating for two years. "It was just what I needed in order to heal myself and think about what I wanted. Only then could I put it out to the universe that I was ready to meet someone," she says.

After her two-year hiatus from dating, Cindy, then thirty-nine, joined a computer dating service affiliated with a religious community organization. Cindy met nine men over a three-month period. One became her husband even though her first reaction was to end the relationship because of his two children from a previous marriage. He persisted, and asked her to give him a fair chance. She explained, "I'd like to have kids so I don't want to go out with a man who already has children. I've been there before." But he still asked her to continue the relationship.

His persistence paid off. Cindy could see he respected her as a professional woman, plus he was open to starting another family. In fact, he was everything she wanted in a man. They met in April, he proposed in September, and they married in May.

Two-thirds of the women we interviewed are currently married, living with, or involved in a significant romantic relationship—startling news for the naysayers who predicted loneliness for women over thirty. Despite their unconventionality as a generation, almost half of Torchbearers who are in relationships have opted to marry. The length of these marriages ranges from one to twenty-seven years with an average of ten years. By examining the marital histories of our sample, we had the opportunity to see if these women are currently involved with men their own age. The answer is an overwhelming "YES." With a few exceptions, Torchbearers appear to prefer men their own age and vice versa—at the time of the interviews, the average age for both the women we interviewed and their male partners was forty-five. Further, most choose partners who match their own level of professional success in similar fields such as law, business, administration, and education.

Old Rule: Do what your mother did because she did it right.

"Even as a child, I don't remember fantasizing about being married and having children. All little girls play house, but I don't remember doing that. I remember playing secretary. I remember playing art gallery owner, but not wife and mother."

Despite an absence of data, the media in the 1980s reported that single women were suffering from record levels of depression. In fact, research shows that single women enjoy better mental health than married women. Single women also make more money, are physically healthier, and are more likely to have regular sex than their married counterparts. Ninety-six percent of the women we interviewed were previously married or lived with a partner at least once, yet one-third were single for some period of time between the ages of thirty-nine and forty-seven. Many of these women found the necessity to be independent for an indefinite period has led to both self-reliance and self-examination, especially when asked, "How come you're not married?"

Judy, a Manhattan-based journalist, has given the subject of marriage a lot of thought. Single at forty-four, her life is in sharp contrast to her mother's and her older sister's, both of whom married at nineteen, had children right away, and never left their small Midwestern hometown. "A lot of us are in our forties and at our peak of everything," Judy told us, "but we're alone. We don't have a man. Given what's out there, being by yourself is better than a bad relationship. After you've been in a few rotten relationships, you realize that having somebody snoring next to you, somebody coming home and asking, 'What's for dinner?' has to be weighed against that old Dorothy Parker line, 'Is the fucking I'm getting worth the fucking I'm getting?' We're the first generation of women who, if the answer is 'No,' have concluded they'd rather be solo."

New Truth: If you choose to do things your own way, ride out your choices.

"Sometimes it seems as though women who don't have a man think they'd be fine if they had one, and vice versa."

The last two decades represent a period in which women made tremendous personal investments in shaping their own futures. Many who were nurturing careers or entering new professions had inordinate demands on their time and energy. The pursuit of job-related goals was a good excuse for those who were still uncertain about personal goals. Lanna is the vice president of a large international bank. At the age of forty, she is grappling with an issue which is not uncommon to women of her generation—her genuine ambivalence about marriage and relationship. "I was engaged once but I was more in love with the idea of getting married than I ever was with him. I was thirty-four and thought, 'It's time to get married. This is what I'm supposed to do.' When we broke up, I wondered if I blew it deliberately," she says.

"When I was twenty-two, I thought I would get married at twenty-five and have my kids before I turned thirty. I just assumed that was the way it was supposed to be. At thirty, my mother had the last of her children; I had none by that age and wasn't even married. Now I've come to terms with the fact that a lot of things haven't turned out the way I expected. Surprisingly, this is fine with me. I was recently asked what I'm most afraid of in life. My biggest fear used to be growing old alone. Now I realize that's not scary. I like the person I've become and I'm very gratified by the friends who are drawn to me and to whom I'm drawn. I'm not alone. I don't have to marry someone if marriage isn't right for me."

Leading-edge baby boomers have the self-perception of eternal youth—some believed that there would always be time to do whatever they want. At forty-two, Colleen optimistically believes that she has three years left to decide if she will have a child. She said, "All through my twenties and thirties I gave lipservice to wanting to get married. When I was thirty-eight, I finally said to myself, 'I don't really want to get married.' In fact, I never wanted to. I just said it because I wanted a child. I always thought it was unfair to have a baby without a husband or partner. If I did, my child would have to live with that decision for the rest of his or her life. Is it fair to put my needs above what's best for another human being?" Whether Colleen has a child or not, she has made sure there will always be children in her life. Still grappling with the decision, she coaches a girls' soccer team and spends considerable time with her nieces and her friends' children.

Old Rule: Have children while you're young.

> *"I wasn't wild about having children. I just didn't see myself as a mother. It was with some ambivalence that I even got pregnant. But when I had that baby it was like some kind of a floodgate opened. It was fantastic."*

By the age of thirty, women historically have completed their family, yet among professional women of the this generation, a sizable percentage postponed their decision to have children until they were considerably older. Many women took a long hard look at their own upbringing and concluded their childhoods were somewhat at odds with Wally and Beaver's experiences. Some were ambivalent about starting a family, afraid they'd replicate the only role models they knew well—their own parents.

For over ten years, Betty and her husband lived a footloose existence in Europe that combined their interests in teaching and travel. What remained unresolved was the "kids, no kids" question. She found herself flowering during those years, enjoying her work, and not at all sure that kids were in the plan. Part of this had to do with Betty's mother who often said that her own children should never have been born. Betty, an only child until she was sixteen years old, recalls going to the doctor with her mother who had mistakenly imagined she had cancer. Betty waited in the car. When her mother returned, she put her head on the steering wheel and cried for twenty minutes. She wouldn't tell Betty what was wrong. Betty later found out that her thirty-six-year-old mother was pregnant. When Betty was a senior in college, her mother, now forty-one years old, got pregnant again. Once more her mother acted as if her life had ended.

After many years of marriage, Betty's husband was ready to start a family. He told her, "If you decide that you don't want children, I'm going to find someone who does." While on vacation in Greece, Betty read *Blackberry Winter* in which Margaret Mead wrote about her joy in having a daughter. This was a turning point for her. She thought, "If Margaret Mead could feel that way about having a child, then maybe I can too. By using one of her icons as a model instead of her own mother, Betty was finally able to say to her husband, 'OK, let's do it.' " Their daughter was born ten months later.

New Truth: Have children, preferably before menopause.

"I began to feel maternal urges in my mid-thirties. I was staring at babies on the street instead of guys."

For many women, the issue of whether to marry has been harder to resolve than the question of children. While women cannot "make" a husband, they can certainly have a baby, with or without a spouse or partner. Today, women may adopt, utilize artificial insemination, or plan conception through sexual intercourse, with the goal being pregnancy rather than marriage. A large percentage of professional baby-boomer women were in their mid- to late-thirties when they first began to seriously consider the idea of having children. As one woman told us, "When I was thirty-nine, I figured that I had three or four years left to have a child."

Sara remarried when she was thirty-eight years old. From the beginning, she and her new husband went back and forth on the matter of children. Her husband had two children from a previous marriage, but he seemed enthusiastic about starting a new family immediately. Sara wanted to wait. Then, her mother died quite suddenly. As they were driving to the funeral, Sara announced, in the mists of her tears, that she wanted to try to get pregnant that day. It horrified her that her mother never had a grandchild and, even worse, that her mother would be nothing more to that child than a name in a story and or a face in a photo album. Sara felt they had to have a baby right away so their child would at least know his or her grandfather. Her husband hesitated. "We go back and forth. If I have children at my age, will I resent them? I've built a comfortable life that I don't necessarily want to change."

On their second anniversary, Sara and her husband learned she was pregnant. They were stunned to realize that they were ecstatic at the news. But Sara miscarried. For over a year, they tried, but when she didn't conceive right away, they became uncertain again. "As time went by, there was more ambivalence and less desire for a child. I had reached the point where if it's meant to be, it will happen." Apparently, it was meant to be. At forty-two, Sara gave birth to a son and now at forty-four, she is pregnant with her second child.

In the 1990s, being an unmarried woman with a child generally has no stigma attached to it. However, other issues must be faced—the necessity of financially supporting a child, the desire to raise a child in an environment with good schools and safe streets, and the ability to find a supportive partner also willing to be a parent. Many unmarried baby boomers grapple with the idea of being a single parent and wonder how exactly to go about getting pregnant.

While elective single parenthood has always been an option, leave it to this generation to come up with a new twist. Although unmarried, Rita, then thirty-five, was certain that she wanted a child. A friend found her a willing and anonymous sperm donor but at the last minute, Rita "chickened out." She thought, "Shouldn't I know where the other half of the genes are coming from?" One of her male friends volunteered to help. They began a sexual relationship with the agreement that if she conceived, Rita would have the baby and he would bear no responsibility. After conceiving her first child in this manner, she decided to have a second child. "This time, I was determined to try artificial insemination. I read about how you could put semen in a turkey baster and do it yourself at home. I thought, 'That sounds right.'" Rita found an agreeable male friend to donate his semen and she conceived. Word spread quickly and she found herself on the informal old-girls lecture circuit explaining the turkey baster method to other women. Several years later, Rita met a wonderful man, fell in love, got married, and, in her forties, had a third child the old-fashioned way.

Old Rule: Normal women want children.

"Why is there such a stigma for a woman to admit that she may not want children?"

Men have always felt free to say they didn't want a family, but despite the gains women have made in the last thirty years, the choice to not have a child raises eyebrows when the speaker is female. Women who are childless by choice are still viewed by some as not quite normal. It is not surprising that support groups are popping up all over the country for women (and men) who are childless by choice. While being single and not having children is one thing, being married, and happily married at that, and choosing to not have children is yet another arena women of this generation have been among the first to enter.

Cora knew that she would not have children. She made the decision to have her tubes tied while she and her husband were childless newlyweds and still in their twenties. Because of their youth, they were required to go through a series of counseling sessions before her doctor would schedule her for surgery. Cora was the oldest child in a large farm family and had cared for her younger siblings. "I had all those mothering instincts put away," she says. Her husband, who was very much anti-children, felt he wouldn't be a good father, so their decision was mutual. Now in her mid-forties, she is sometimes asked if she has had second thoughts. "Honestly, no," she answers. "I like holding babies, but I like sending them home at the end of the day. My mother had a problem with our decision. She felt hurt and thought that she didn't raise me right. I told her, 'I just don't think I could do as good a job as you.' That really didn't come into it; I just didn't want kids." Cora and her husband have been married for twenty years and say they have never regretted their decision.

New Truth: Sometimes normal women don't have children.

"Do I have something to grieve over that I don't know about? I don't feel sad. I feel pissed off because I got left out of something that I won't get to experience as a woman."

It has been reported that as many as 30 percent of women born after 1944 will remain permanently childless and 25 percent of all boomer women will have only one child. Many of these women postponed marriage, never married, or delayed child-bearing until it was too late to have children of their own. Others married young, divorced before they had children, and remarried later in life. According to a *Fortune* magazine article, "The way a second marriage differs most dramatically from the first can be summed up in a single word, 'children.' There usually aren't any." An astounding 50 percent of the women we interviewed are childless and 20 percent have only one child. Only one in twenty have three or more natural and/or adopted children. A sizable percentage of Torchbearers are parenting their husband's children from a former marriage (22 percent) with two step-children being typical.

Decisions about marriage and family that were once made automatically are now very carefully thought through. Melanie chose not to have a child although she has been married to her high-school sweetheart for almost twenty-five years. She questioned her husband's ability to parent based on her experience with her own father who took little responsibility for his children. "My father never changed a diaper," she says. "He was a workaholic and my brother, who committed suicide in his twenties, suffered because of that. For me, one of the most wonderful sights in the world is to see a father actively participating in bringing up his children. I don't know if my husband has that in him. Some people ask, 'If you had a child, how do you know your husband wouldn't make the time to parent?' The answer is that I don't know." Like many women with busy careers of their own, Melanie decided she could not work full-time and raise a child without considerable support from her spouse. When she concluded that her husband's participation would be minimal, she elected not to have a family.

Old Rule: Normal women have children the normal way.

"In my thirties, I really wanted a baby. I even bought books of baby names but then I lost interest. It wasn't conscious, I was busy doing too many other things. Then it got to the point where I thought, 'I'm just too old.'"

Joan's first husband, whom she married in her mid-twenties, was arrested several times for suspected pedophilia. The idea of having children in that marriage was unthinkable. After her divorce, she seriously believed she would never remarry, yet she remained ambivalent about children. She says, "I went through a period when I wanted a child and then a period when I didn't." On her fortieth birthday, still single, she acknowledged that she had reached the point where it just wasn't going to happen.

Two and one-half years later, at a baseball game, she met her future husband. She says, "He's very easy going, much calmer than I am. I feel like I have this wonderful blanket wrapped around me." Last year on Valentine's Day, Joan and her husband went to dinner at a romantic restaurant. They were seated next to a couple who appeared to be in their late thirties or early forties. At the table with them was a baby, perhaps three months old. The happy couple was thrilled with their baby and seemed very much in love. To Joan, they looked like a commercial. She says, "I looked at them and I started to cry. It took me completely by surprise because I was having a wonderful evening. I thought, 'How can I be so out of touch?' I cried because I would never know what it was like to have my own baby. It's something that I've missed out on and that's painful." Although she felt sad for several days, Joan said the incident brought some closure for her. "This is the last time that I am going to deal with that," she says hopefully.

New Truth: There is more than one way to have children.

"I was taking my temperature and using these ovulation kits. I called the clinic and said, 'I'll be ovulating tomor-

*row.' I went into the clinic and boom, just like that, I was
pregnant. I thought it was going to take months. The clinic
was very surprised. They said, 'You're off the charts for the
law of averages.' I felt like Dr. Frankenstein."*

Jill and her husband are considering adoption. At forty-one, Jill
wants children. An active aunt in her sister's family, Jill has been
at the birth of all three nephews whom she calls "my three boys."
In her thirties, Jill had two miscarriages with the man she lived
with before she met her husband. She got pregnant on their
honeymoon but miscarried yet again. After that, she started
doing what she calls "the fertility number." The first doctor she
consulted said she was not a good case because of her history of
fibroid surgeries and chronic endometriosis. Unwilling to give
up, she consulted with another fertility specialist, but she still
was unable to conceive. For over a year, she and her husband
followed the tedious routine of drugs and shots without success.
Jill told us, "We went through in vitro procedures during the first
year of our marriage which didn't work and negatively affected
our sexual relationship. When I entered the first stages of
menopause, I realized I would never have a natural child. I suggested to my husband that we adopt. We have a lot to give, not
just financially, but emotionally and intellectually. We have
plans to adopt a child this year."

When Mary and Bill started going out together in 1981, she
told him on the first date that she didn't want to get involved
with a man who had a vasectomy. They married after Bill readily agreed to have his vasectomy reversed. For eight years, they
tried to get pregnant, but nothing happened. A fertility special-

ist told them her husband's low sperm count was the problem. If Mary wanted to get pregnant, it would have to be through artificial insemination. Mary and Bill took a break from trying to think over the hard news. Years went by and they were still taking a break. With Bill's encouragement, Mary made an appointment with another fertility specialist. Mary describes the in vitro experience as "so intense that the more you can't have a baby, the more you want one." Throughout, she tried to remain philosophical. She thought, "If it works, it works." Her daughter was born when Mary was forty-three years old.

Old Rule: If you love a man, you'll love his children and they'll love you.

> *"I married Tom and moved into a ready-made family. I went from being a single woman in Chicago to a mother of two in rural Montana. I was responsible for a five- and a six-year-old when I had no experience with children whatsoever. Plus, they came to me rather badly bent, although I had no gauge to know what was normal."*

Many of the women we interviewed are in relationships with divorced men, and a significant number are raising children from their husbands' previous marriages. Because these women have overcome so many professional and personal hurdles in life, some naively believed they could cope with step-parenting as they have with everything else. Instead, many found that being a step-parent can be both difficult and disappointing. Sonya's husband had been divorced for four years when they met. Sonya confesses that she has little emotional attachment to her step-children. She honestly admits, "I'm not wild about them. Their attitude is, 'What can daddy do for me? What will daddy buy me? Where will daddy take me?' His birthday came and went without even a card from his children. The hardest part is that I feel in the middle. For my husband's sake, I want them to be these great kids he has a terrific relationship with. He makes excuses about their behavior because he needs to keep himself going, whereas I don't make excuses for their irritating behavior. I try not to be negative but, the truth is, they piss me off."

Mae married at thirty-two. Her husband was eight years older and had two daughters, three and eight. She was so much in love that she assumed things would just work out. She didn't think about the reality of raising two young children who were not her own. Immediately after their marriage, her new husband and his children moved in with her. Mae's house was small and after living alone for so many years, the adjustment was difficult. "I felt totally encroached upon," she recalls. "I went from complete freedom to no freedom. I never had my husband to myself. All of a sudden, I became this *mother*. I had all these ideas about how children should behave and how a family should be. The fact is that they didn't like doing the things that I liked to do. I was nothing to them, yet I couldn't back off."

Dad wants step-mom to participate in his children's lives, but this often translates into dad dispensing the discipline, leaving step-mom responsible for everyday activities such as cooking meals, grocery shopping, clothes buying, and planning events for the weekends. In Mae's situation, the more daily maintenance she did, the more resentment she felt from the children. Since both biological parents were "pretty hang loose," if anyone were going to interfere, it was Mae, the iron-handed step-mother. To this day, she feels that this affected her relationship with his children.

New Truth: Being a step-parent means being a wise friend.

"I'm the luckiest step-parent in the world. I feel like I had a family without the stretch marks."

Some Torchbearers married older men, particularly those women who divorced early or postponed marriage in order to pursue their careers. Although Fran always assumed she would be a mother someday, her husband made it clear, as a condition of their relationship, that there would be no children. After more than a decade of marriage, Fran still wonders about her future, given the likelihood that she will be alone at some point because her husband is twenty years her senior. She realizes, however, that not all children are a great comfort to their parents, including her own siblings and herself. She also knows it's a bad reason to have children if the expectation is that someone will take care of you someday. Her decision to marry an older man who did not wish to raise a second family meant giving up having a child of her own and, at twenty-five, becoming a step-mother to two teenage children instead.

Fran met her husband, who was her professor, in graduate school. "We couldn't tell anybody," she recalls. "The whole thing seemed very secretive, which was exciting and fun. The only problem was his children. What was my role there? I was closer in age to them than to my husband. I wasn't a mother and I wasn't a sister. You can't be friends because they don't want you to be a friend. It's taken years, but I'm pleased to say that I don't have that struggle anymore. We have become close. My relationship with my step-son has its ups and downs. After all these years, he is still trying to figure out who we are to each other. It's confusing for all blended families." Today, when Fran looks at women in their twenties, she says to her husband, "I can't believe you thought I could handle two teenagers at that age." Fran, now forty-one, has recently completed a law degree. As her husband contemplates retirement, she is looking forward to beginning her new career.

Countless women who never had a family of their own have thrived in the role of step-parent. Although Jill's first marriage lasted a dozen years, there were no children, partially due to problems with drugs and alcohol. Today, sober and thriving as a college administrator, she shares her home and life with a man fifteen years her senior. She told us, "My boyfriend has a big family and I love it. He has five children and ten grandchildren whom I adore. All of a sudden, I find myself in the midst of this huge family which has welcomed me. They call me Grandma. It's very clever of me to become a grandmother without having gone through the trials and tribulations of motherhood. I do all the right things that grandmothers should do. I spoil them rotten, buy them gifts, undermine their parents, and then send them home."

Many women have developed warm, loving relationships with their partner's children over time. Molly considers herself blessed. She describes her step-daughter as her closest friend in the world which Molly, in typical boomer fashion, attributes to pure luck. As a recovering addict, Molly proudly says that neither of her twenty-something step-children drinks or uses drugs. Although she is completely turned on by who they are as young adults and how they have chosen to direct their lives, she freely admits that this wasn't always the case. When she first met their father, they were eight and nine. At that time, Molly was in the initial stages of recovery and had no interest in children or much else for that matter.

"Whenever I'm around infants for a day or two, I have some dreams about having a baby," she says. "If those dreams had lasted, I might have changed my mind, but they just went away. If I didn't have such a close relationship with my step-children perhaps I would feel differently. Maybe if I didn't have such a great dog I would feel differently. I am part of a family, so there isn't anything missing. The maternal urge was never very strong even when I was younger. I remember being ten or twelve and wondering, 'If there are so many unwanted children in the world, why should you have your own? Why can't you just take a needy child and raise it?' I guess that's what I've done, taken the people who are around me and made them my children."

Real life in the '90s

> *"Many Torchbearers have opted, for one reason or another, not to embark on conventional family lives."*

In 1962, Helen Gurley Brown shocked the world by announcing, "Nice girls do have affairs and they do not necessarily die of them." Baby boomers are the first generation to test this out and put to rest old notions about propriety, modesty, restraint, and a pristine past as requisites for niceness. Carol Gilligan has proposed that the conflict between self and others constitutes the central moral dilemma for women. She writes, "The 'good woman' masks assertion, claiming only to meet the needs of others; the 'bad woman' forgoes or renounces commitments." One woman told us, "I have a permanent sexually transmittable disease. It's been difficult to reconcile having this disease with my self image. I remember crying when my doctor told me. I kept saying to myself, 'But I'm a nice girl.' And I am a nice girl...with a permanent sexually transmittable disease. That's the point. A nice girl had abortions. A nice girl had an affair with a married man. A nice girl drank too much for too many years. A nice girl did a lot of things. So here we are, living with these contradictions. On paper, this doesn't look very good, but maybe our generation has redefined 'nice.'"

Little in the average woman's life encourages within her a willingness to risk, yet those who do have much to gain from having taken the risk. Torchbearers have broken from tradition more than they allow themselves to see, particularly with regard to their personal choices which have rocked the social fabric of the country. Again and again, they have demonstrated their capacity to make successive and successful connections in an unpredictable and changing world. As these women move into the new millennium, they will undoubtedly continue to rock the boat.

Chapter Seven

I've Grown, What's His Problem?

"My husband is trying to decide if he's comfortable with the person I've become. I'm not a passive 'Yes honey, anything you want' kind of woman. The only way men of our generation are going to change is if we keep changing ourselves. I told him, if you say, 'Stay at point A, don't go to point B,' I'm immediately going to point B. He has to understand that my goal is to keep going: B, C, D, E, F. If he wants to come along, fine, but I can't be dragged back. I'm a woman and I'm growing."

Almost without exception, Torchbearers feel they have changed more than men their age. Barbara Ehrenrich writes that, "In the 1970s, it became an article of liberal faith that a new man would eventually rise up to match the new feminist woman, that he would be more androgynous than any 'old' variety of man—an evolutionary leap from John Wayne to Alan Alda." But the "New Man" did not arise.

Many women had relationships with men of their generation that didn't work out. They either fell in love with an unavailable man, discovered that the man of their dreams was a horrible husband, or married someone they didn't love. After experiencing considerable pain and sadness, coupled with periods of self-examination and insight, they made the difficult decision to leave. In this chapter, four women recall how they broke the old rules of "Stand by your man" and " 'Til death do us part" and came to the hard-won realization that they deserved healthy, loving life partners. The process of ending bad relationships with unworthy husbands or lovers enabled them to move on with their lives and make more satisfying and appropriate choices in the future.

Old Rule: Stand by your man.

"Stand by your man," a popular country-western song from the late '60s, stands in stark contrast to the message of the women's liberation movement. How did women of this generation reconcile the contradiction between their childhood teaching that the most important adult task for a woman was to find a man to take care of her and the reality that she could take care of herself? Because of these conflicting expectations, many chose to marry simply because it was "time." A surprising number of women quickly discerned that they had become involved with the wrong man, but chose to stay in the relationship anyway. Others found out later that the man of their dreams was no bargain. Still others were led astray by their partners, trusting in them, and giving up their own power. When they were ready to leave these unhappy or destructive relationships, they were fortunate to have the support of their friends and, in many cases, the financial resources from their own careers to break away.

Because so many accounts of abusive and deceitful men were shared, we begin this chapter with four stories about love gone awry. These stories parallel what many women have experienced, perhaps to a lesser extent, when they realized they had fallen in love with the wrong man. By sharing their stories, we offer hope to women of all ages to challenge dysfunctional patterns and dead-end relationships.

"I really never wanted to be anything. I just wanted to fall in love, get married, and have a family."

Lorraine had few career aspirations after college, so she was footloose and available to fall in love with a bald-headed, bearded, New Age guru. They traveled together in a Volkswagen van to every hippie gathering on the West Coast. "I consciously tried to do everything my parents never exposed me to," Lorraine says. "When I met Govinda, I left them in the dust. My world opened up."

But Lorraine's life wasn't nirvana. Govinda was arrogant, narcissistic, and noncommittal. His actions constantly reminded her of his "open relationship" beliefs. He told her, "You can't possibly expect me to learn and grow in all the ways I need if I only have sex with one woman." For four years, Lorraine went along with a situation she neither liked nor found acceptable, simply because she was in love. "I would come home and find Govinda in our bed with another woman. When we traveled, I'd reach over to touch him at night and he'd be gone. He would be making love with some stranger in the hot tub." Finally, during a three-month New Age healing festival, Govinda's behavior so enraged Lorraine that she left him. She returned home and got a job, but they reconciled and continued to live together for two more years. "He was very bad for me, but I just couldn't let the relationship go," she says.

New Truth: Life turns out in ways you never expected.

Eventually, Lorraine got fed up, left Govinda, and decided to go back to school. "I went to the library and looked up graduate school programs. There was one program in public administration, an area of study I had never even heard of. Nonetheless, I applied and got accepted with a full scholarship. Once I was back in school, I got back into my capable mode and eventually earned a master's degree. One day, I was walking by a bulletin board—I'm stressing this because truly my career was by default—and saw a notice for a government management intern program." Lorraine applied and went for an interview. "I made a speech, led a group discussion, and did whatever they asked me to do. Somehow I got accepted! When I returned home, my girl-friend picked me up at the airport. I was still dressed in my inter-view uniform, a blue suit with high heels. We went to a bar, ordered a drink, clicked glasses, and I made a toast to myself. 'From now on everything will change,' I said. I knew then that the New Age thing was over for me. Now that I have top secu-rity clearance in my job, my life has become very circumspect and conventional."

Lorraine's earliest aspiration was to marry and have chil-dren, but she fell in love and found herself living communally with other New Age seekers. Regardless of all the alternative lifestyle routes she took, the one thing Lorraine wanted most, a committed relationship, eluded her. The downside of social and sexual experimentation was that many people got hurt. Lorraine was one of them. Now a successful consultant who travels extensively, she is still searching for a loving relationship. Like many women of this generation, Lorraine got exactly what she didn't anticipate—a meaningful career, financial rewards, and independence. She also regained the self-worth she set aside in her relationship with the wrong man.

> *"I felt like I was his romantic, sexual wife and she was his mothering, nurturing wife. It seemed to work very well for him, although neither she nor I were particularly pleased with the situation."*

Judy, an attractive financial planner in her thirties, began seeing a man she'd met at work who had what he described as an open marriage. She fell completely in love with Hal, and despite his refusal to divorce his wife, they remained in a long-term relationship for twelve years. He told Judy he would ask for a trial separation, but six weeks later, his wife, who knew he was seeing another woman, announced that she was pregnant. After his wife became pregnant a second time, Judy ended the relationship, but her resolve wasn't strong and she reconciled with Hal once again. When his wife discovered that they were still seeing each other, she insisted Hal call Judy and end the relationship forever. But the drama was not over. Hal's wife began calling Judy at home and at work. "She called my boss and my secretary and told them I was a terrible person. She even threatened my physical safety," Judy says.

New Truth: Protect yourself.

Judy finally grew tired of the situation and told Hal about his wife's threats. She said, "If you're not going to protect me, I'll protect myself. I will not allow you to sit silently while she castigates me. If you are that spineless, I will reveal everything you ever said or did. I have every love letter you ever sent me. I will tell her I know about every marriage counseling session you went to and that I was the one who gave you the name of the therapist. I will tell her you got me pregnant. She's mad at me, but she's angry at the wrong person. You've lied to her and she's lied to herself. This is your problem now, not mine."

She spoke to Hal only once more after that, but he was very distant. He told her he would tell his wife the whole truth. Judy replied, "'Which truth is that? The one you told me or the one you want her to hear? You've been living two truths and I'm not sure which one is right.' I was devastated, but it was also the most releasing experience I've ever had. I was chained to him emotionally for so long, but I got over him pretty damn fast. I thought it would take years.

"Within a month, I was in the best and happiest place in my life, comfortable with myself and my friends. I didn't feel the need to have a man in my life. My freedom was handed back to me, a huge gift that I didn't know I was going to get. It has been wonderful. Recently, I started to date a very nice man. If he stays in my life I'll be happy, but if he doesn't, I won't be as devastated as I was before. I feel released now that Hal and his wife are out of my life." Lorraine and Judy both experienced the pain of being in love with men in "open" relationships, although from opposite positions. In the next stories, relationship problems surfaced within traditional marriages.

"Everybody was against me marrying him: my parents, my friends, everybody—and my male friends in particular."

In college, Dee became involved in both the anti-war and women's rights movements. Through these activities, she met Ed, a fellow activist who became her husband. "It was a tumultuous relationship; we were always breaking up and getting back together. Ed comes from a fairly dysfunctional family. His mother never hid the fact that she didn't want her only son to marry."

After Dee landed her first job as a reporter, she and Ed decided to marry, mainly because they had been dating for so long. They postponed the wedding twice because each time the wedding day approached, Dee would develop a terrible rash and have to be hospitalized. "I didn't realize what my body was telling me, but I had a terrible sense of dread," she said. "When I would try to talk about how I felt, my family and friends would say, 'Everybody is nervous before getting married. It's normal.' On my wedding day, as I was waiting to walk down the aisle with my father, I sobbed that I couldn't go through with the wedding. My father told me that I had a choice, but all I could think of was the 250 people waiting for me and the money my parents had spent. My father said, 'I don't care who's here or how much money I spent. Don't do it!' All of a sudden, I just plunged ahead of him and he had to catch up. I should never have gone through with that marriage."

The man who seemed so liberated and marched with her for equal rights suddenly became a very old-fashioned husband. "I made the money," Dee says, "but he paid the bills and gave me an allowance. Everything was my responsibility—the car, the laundry, the shopping. I chose this man, but I felt like he tricked me.

"One day, I got a call from the police department saying that my husband had been arrested. I thought it was some terrible mistake. I left work and drove to the police station. Two women said he had followed them in his car and exposed himself. Because they were lesbians, Ed maintained that he didn't do anything and that they just hated men. Since there had never been any hint of anything like this before, I naively believed him. The police let him go because the women saw me sobbing and decided not to press charges."

But the problems began to intensify. "Constant fighting. Lots of passive-aggressive behavior. He'd make me late for work on purpose. He'd take the car to run an errand that would take ten minutes, but he'd be gone for an hour. I thought he was having an affair. I later found out that not only was he driving around exposing himself, but he also was having an affair!" Dee started counseling because she wanted to leave the marriage. Her husband agreed to therapy as well, but stopped after two sessions. While he was out of town for a job interview, Dee got a phone call. Ed had been arrested again, this time for driving near a school yard and exposing himself. She remembers, "I had to borrow money on my credit card to pay the bail. Driving home, Ed told me that it was all my fault because our sex life wasn't satisfying."

New Truth: Trust your intuition about men.

Although Dee felt embarrassed and ashamed that she had "made such a stupid mistake" in marrying Ed, she eventually built up the courage, told her parents, and divorced. Many years later, Dee still gets angry at herself. "I look back and it seems like I'm watching a movie," she says. "It's remarkable that as strong as I am, I allowed this to happen. I shouldn't say that I allowed it, because I had a choice: I participated in it." Dee views her life as more settled now. She owns a lucrative business, works on various political campaigns, and volunteers with Planned Parenthood. In terms of relationships, her tolerance level has definitely changed. "I still choose unconventional men, but over time they've been healthier, more established, and more respectful of me. I have learned to trust my intuition in my relationships with men," she says.

> *"The truth is, I knew I shouldn't marry him. But I felt I could sacrifice to get what I wanted, which was a family."*

Peggy was a successful entrepreneur in her mid-thirties when she met and married Don. Although her life was very full, she wanted to have a child so she married her best prospect. She closed her company and moved to New York at his insistence, giving up her work contacts, friendships, and family support. According to Peggy, "He talked me into moving and then left town the day I moved in. I eventually started a new company, but most of the time I was alone and miserable. My husband was involved with a human potential group which I grew to hate. I had no idea how tied he was to that cult. It could be four in the morning, but if the head honcho called, he'd jump out of bed and leave on the spot. If we were on vacation and he was instructed to come home, we'd be on the next plane out. I went into therapy my first year of marriage because I was so unhappy."

In their second year of marriage, her husband moved to Paris to head the group's European division. He came home only one weekend a month. Peggy, who was pregnant at the time, had no idea her husband was living with his new French girlfriend. In her sixth month, Peggy learned that her unborn son had no kidneys. "I had a 103 degree fever for ten days and my life was in jeopardy so they had to terminate the pregnancy. My husband returned home, but he didn't come to be with me. He told me he never wanted the baby and announced he was filing for divorce as soon as I got out of the hospital. This was the most horrible time of my life.

"A month after the pregnancy was terminated, I began hemorrhaging badly. He happened to be at home but wouldn't take me to the emergency room. He said, 'It's just your period.' He finally brought me to the hospital, but only after we stopped at Denny's so he could have breakfast first. When I walked into the emergency room, a nurse said, 'Get a doctor immediately, this woman is bleeding to death.' The staff couldn't believe it had taken so long for me to get help." After Peggy lost her son and separated from her husband, she developed insomnia and became deeply depressed. With great difficulty, she managed to keep her business afloat.

But her husband claimed partial ownership of Peggy's busi-ness as part of the divorce settlement, asserting that half her assets were his. Because he was in Europe, her lawyers couldn't subpoena him. "We couldn't touch him," she recalls. "He hired the meanest lawyers who assaulted me with requests for every check I had ever written. He ended up with half of my business, half of my car, half of my savings, and half of my retirement account."

New Truth: Don't settle for a man who is less than you deserve.

After the divorce, Peggy kept thinking, "God, why are you keeping me here?" To heal, she rented a condo by the ocean where she could relax and recuperate. Eventually, she moved her business, bought a house, and began a new relationship. "I'm in the rebuilding stage. It's very difficult, but I have a stronger foundation now and I am more grounded," Peggy told us. "My life before Don was very good. My business has survived, but even if I were to lose it, I'd be OK. I'm angry at times, but I've come through the worst. As shocking and horrible as the situation was, being pregnant gave me more insight into the wonder and awe of my own body. Do I want children? Yes. Will I have children? I don't know."

New Truth: Life beyond bad relationships begins with awareness.

What can we learn from these accounts? Lorraine, Judy, Dee, and Peggy were actors in their own dramas. Each woman acknowledges her own complicity in choosing a partner who was bad for her and then giving her power away to someone who used and abused it. Ironically, many Torchbearers who became more liberated in work were far less liberated in love and intimacy. While they may have had a more adventurous sex life than women of previous generations, they were not yet freed from deep unconscious patterns of relating to men or of defining themselves in terms of their relationships.

Women in this generation straddle two worlds—the world of their mothers and the world of liberation. As children, they learned how a woman was to behave with a man from observing their mothers who saw fulfillment in being a good wife, who depended financially on their husbands, and who defined themselves by their martial status. Lorraine, Judy, Dee, and Peggy followed their early programming and became involved with men they hoped would fulfill their childhood images. But when the relationships failed, these women, as good girls, blamed themselves for being stupid or gullible.

Otherwise-liberated women stay in bad relationships because they naively think they can make things better if only they do more, act differently, hang in there, look the other way, or smooth conflict over. An unfortunate legacy for some is self-doubt that has its roots in early relationships with men who behaved badly. Through psychotherapy, consciousness-raising groups, and talking candidly with other women—things their mothers did not do—they learned that their worth went beyond what these men thought of them. More than that, these women learned that they had given away something they could take back—their personal power. After much hard work, they regained control over their lives and reclaimed their hearts. Were these men all Big Bad Wolves waiting to prey on innocent

Little Red Riding Hoods? Were they ogres who used the women who loved them? Yes and no.

Like their female counterparts, baby-boomer men were the beneficiaries and victims of their times. Many men of this generation were raised by Depression-era parents in households with the submissive female/dominant male model. Their male image was of a warrior father who was not demonstrably close to either his wife or his children—as sons, they absorbed this message. Unlike their fathers, these men had the option to modify their rigid beliefs and adjust their behavior, but they rarely did. When the culture began to shift, many men could not keep up with the ways in which women were changing. "They slowed down," says one woman. "They didn't grow as far away from their fathers as they could have. Men couldn't be John Wayne anymore. They couldn't swagger into a room and grab some woman like a prize. What were they supposed to do now? They couldn't play out situations the way they used to. Men never had an organized movement or an ideology, as women did, to help them figure out who they are supposed to be."

Because Torchbearers' fundamental needs were not being met under the old '50s model, they were motivated to access resources for change and take advantage of new opportunities. The cost of challenging old beliefs and patterns was that many relationships had to end in order for these women to thrive. Teresa told us, "Men of this generation are paying the price for all the oppression that was perpetrated on women under the old model that we rejected. Women woke up and said, 'Either change or I'm leaving.' Men have to become better human beings. They have to put their money where their mouth is about their egalitarianism or they're going to end up alone or in lousy relationships." Unlike men their age, Torchbearers let go of their childhood "shoulds" and saw myriad possibilities for themselves. As a result, they created a major shift in women's consciousness by acting on this awareness. But what happened to the men?

Are there male Torchbearers?

"Never before has a generation of men been faced with such a challenge to their sense of adequacy and masculinity. Raised by doting mothers to be the stalwart providers who would be desired and accepted by compliant women, they reached marriageable ages in a new era of independent, achieving women who demand equitable partnership status in marriage rather than the old lord and master of the house set-up. Like victims of the technological revolution, these men were trained for jobs that have suddenly been eliminated."

—Carol Smith, author

Barbara Ehrenrich, in *Remaking Love*, writes about the much-anticipated New Man who would emerge, freed of past cultural and social shackles, in response to the transformed New Woman. What this New Man would look like has been the subject of much discussion. In the '80s, Alan Alda and Phil Donahue were frequently mentioned as prototypes. Anne Taylor Fleming, in *Motherhood Deferred*, describes the New Man as "a charmingly off-putting sexual revolution hybrid with a kind of passive-aggressive masculinity."

The New Man surfaced in popular psychology books as a little boy in men's clothing who, like Peter Pan, refuses to grow up. He is also described as a victim of the New Woman who has both sexually and economically emasculated him. Ideally, he is depicted as an egalitarian man who supports his wife, shares in household and family responsibilities, and communicates openly with his partner. Does the New Man exist? We wondered and asked the women we interviewed whether they had observed changes in men equal to their own.

Without a doubt, women think a lot about men. Overall, they like men, live with men, and want men in their lives. They are neither "man-haters" or "male-bashers" nor do they have unrealistic expectations for finding a custom-fit man in an off-the-rack world. Yet, women are very critical of the men of their generation for not changing as much as they have. Dana, married for nineteen years, sees herself as the one who has borne the weight of the relationship. "I've carried the burden of most of the finances, most of the child raising, and most of the house-keeping. My husband admires that very much, but he's also frightened by it. My life insists that he change now if we're to stay together. He gets rebellious and resentful about women like me pressing for change out of our own need to go forward. Men don't seem to have that same need."

While some males treat women fairly, the majority of women we interviewed felt that many men still expect, and demand, traditional female behavior of their wives and colleagues. "None of the men I know do the housework or child care to the same extent as their wives," one woman says. "Yet, men consistently misconceive their contribution as being equal.

Possibly that's because they're doing 10 percent more than their fathers ever did."

Because men have been in the alpha dog position for so long, they have little motivation to alter their behavior. As one woman says, "A lot of men want to keep the status quo because they're the ones who stand to gain by protecting it. Women were thrust into the psychological understanding that they had to change, but men didn't think they had to because they were already in the superior position. They never learned to stop doing things that are oppressive to women."

Many women of this generation express anger, disappointment, or bitterness about this state of affairs, particularly in terms of its effect on women at home and in the workplace. Gail, a college professor, says, "There's probably a correlation between the amount of violence against women, both physical and psychological, and women's advancement in careers and in the world. Each of us has been under attack at one time or another by a man because we were trying to do a good job or trying to be a self-actualized, independent person. There's not a woman anywhere who has escaped criticism and psychological or physical violence for trying to better herself."

By reviewing the transcripts of the interviews, we were able to identify three distinct types of men: The Traditional Man, who is still trying to live the life of his father; the Surface Change Man, who talks the talk but doesn't walk the walk; and the New Man, who is committed to creating mutually supportive relationships both at home and at work. Having had experiences with all three types, many are cautiously optimistic about the future of male-female relationships.

The Traditional Man a.k.a. "Mr. Man"

"A lot of men wish they could embrace a bimbo. Life would be so simple. They're like Southern plantation own-ers after the Civil War. Are they going to sit around talk-ing about how great it was before the war or are they going to get with it?"

"Men have not changed very much." We heard this from count-less women, although their reasons differ. Julie attributes men's recalcitrance to their personalities, "They're not self-reflective. They think that if they ignore an issue long enough, it will go away. Men are not sensitive, they don't nurture like women do, and they don't worry about whether they are hurting someone else's feelings. But since men are an important part of the equa-tion, we can't ignore them. Still it's far-fetched for a woman like me to say, 'Oh, honey, you're so *strong*; you're just so *brilliant*. Why didn't I think of that?'"

Beth, a software developer, proposes that egalitarian rela-tionships are the exception rather than the rule because so many men have trouble letting go of their traditional perceptions about a woman's role. "Men still have the attitude that a woman is supposed to work full-time, then come home and cook, clean, and take care of the baby," she says. "It's out of balance to expect a woman to handle two full-time jobs, one in the home and one outside, and not have fifty-fifty participation from her male part-ner. I resent that and other women do too."

Some are highly critical of the forces which try to keep women in their place. Mary Ellen fears the situation has worsened, "I don't see any evidence of men being more egalitarian. If anything, they take great pride in pointing out where women who have pursued their own goals failed. The success of the political Right and the popularity of conservative talk shows are evidence of that, as well as the increasing violence against women. There are probably the same number of men who are congenial toward women today as there were in the past. If anything, there's been a backlash."

Another woman looks to history as a source of men's inability to see women as equal partners. "Men say the same things over and over, but nothing changes. I have put everything on the line to make major changes in my life, so I have a lot of trouble with their failure to act. I've studied how the male has interpreted female sexuality in history as a negative or threatening essence of the devouring mother—hardly a cultural image that promotes positive, equal relationships." Brenda sees a lot of bravado in men and a need to have their accomplishments recognized. "Men see themselves as the breadwinners," she says. "They're going to get this job or climb that mountain. They're going to be President of the United States! Meanwhile, as women, we have to fight for everything and prove ourselves ten times more than men. Something inside us has made us achieve. As a result, women are stronger than ever. We're good at what we do but we're quiet about it. Men are never quiet about it."

The Surface Change Man a.k.a. "Big King Daddy Rabbit"

"Men like my husband talk a good game about women and men being equal, but they don't act on it. When we talk

about my earning more money than he does, he says, 'Oh no, that isn't threatening to me.' But when we talk about having children, he says he's not going to mess with stuff like changing diapers. God forbid! That's my job."

The women we interviewed repeatedly say that many men their age appear to be supportive of women on the outside, but underneath, they remain the same old traditional guys. "Men are just realizing how much women have changed," Donna told us. "If they don't start to change themselves, they're going to end up like Senator Packwood who claims that it was 'devil alcohol' that drove him to denigrate the women who worked for him. As long as he supported the feminist movement publicly, he didn't have to change inside. Men like him felt it was enough to make a contribution to Ms. magazine and say they support women's issues. But internal change? Forget it. The men who give lip service are just as oppressive as men who are overtly suppressive of women."

Even women who acknowledge that there has been some change continue to express concern about men's inability to take responsibility at home. "I went through years and years of relationships with terrific men, but even so, I felt like I was doing day care with them. I had to train each one and teach him what it meant to be in a relationship that was equal and fair, with shared power, responsibility, and communication. Men of our generation may have changed the way they style their hair or the way they dress. Some even changed the type of work they do and the amount of time they devote to their community, but at home, it is the same old story."

Criticism about the degree to which men have changed echoes through a number of comments. One Torchbearer says, "A friend said she was marrying her boyfriend not only because he would go out and buy toilet paper, but he actually noticed when they ran out. When men go to the supermarket and buy household items without women having to remind them, I'll believe we've made progress." Another woman views her husband as enlightened, but finds that the older he gets, the more traditional he becomes. "This is very disappointing. He'll phone home while he's away on a business trip and say, 'I called the other night and you weren't home. Where were you?' I tell him, 'Honey, I've got my own life. I'm doing my thing.'"

> "When I tell a man that I own a highly successful business, he says, 'Great! That's wonderful. You should really be proud of yourself.' Inside he's thinking, 'God, she's so independent. She's being paged when we're out to dinner. I don't know if I can handle that.' Then I never hear from him again."

Not only have baby-boomer men made few substantive changes in the domestic arena, but they have difficulty being with women who are more successful than they are or supporting women in their professional activities. Colleen, a doctor who eventually divorced her husband, says, "My husband initially was very pro-women and egalitarian on the surface. Even though he knew my career was very important to me, he demanded that I give it up and work part-time. He couldn't tolerate my having a successful career. He actually said, 'I want you to be here when

I get home. I want my dinner prepared. I want someone to bring me my slippers. I want all these things.' I give him credit for being so honest, but I told him, 'I would like to be able to do some of those things, but I resent your demanding that I do them. I can't live up to your picture of a wife.' I tried to tell him that he had to see all of me, not just my loving and domestic side, but he just couldn't."

Rachel, a conference planner, recalls that her new husband wanted an energetic, professional person like her—that is, until after they married. "He's had to come to grips with the reality of who I am," Rachael admits. "He's better about it now, but before it was threatening to him when I was working or talking on the phone at night. Sometimes he'll ask me how my day went, but he doesn't ask in-depth questions. Maybe it's about competition. He dislikes my work side and says I'm too uptight when I get home at night. In my previous relationship, my boyfriend was also my mentor so we talked about work all the time. Rather, he talked and I listened. But at least I had some dialogue with a man about my career. Now I don't, so it's been frustrating."

Some women choose not to marry because they don't believe men are capable of supporting them through their challenging work careers. A corporate executive, who has a long-time male companion whom she doesn't live with, says, "Why are CEO women single? The men who are their equals are married. Few men are willing to be the nurturer, the supporter, the mate-on-the-arm—all things that someone in an influential position needs. When you chip away at the surface, many men still really want a traditional wife. My significant other is a non-traditional man, but when his needs get pushed back because of my work responsibilities—which involve evenings out, long hours, travel, and deadlines—his inclination is to want a more traditional relationship."

One woman half-facetiously told us, "At one time I wanted a well-built man who would be there when I come home at night, make my dinner, and be wonderful in bed. The traditional wife, only male." She later abandoned the search.

The New Man a.k.a. "The Egalitarian Man"

"Among the couples we know, the relationships seem pretty equal. There doesn't seem to be any underlying authoritarian bones in these men."

Generally speaking, women who feel their partner is a New Man acknowledge that he is an exception because he was raised differently, he comes from another culture, he's learned from his mistakes in a previous relationship, he's unique, he's older, or he's younger. "I don't have a single friend in a bad marriage," says Roberta. "That must be my choice. I wouldn't tolerate a friend who put herself in a position where she was held back or made to feel small. My husband and all of my friends' husbands are doing the best they can. They're putting out a lot of effort to be the kind of men that we need them to be."

"All my friends envy me because they don't have a husband like mine," says Elaine. "My husband does more of the women stuff around the house than I do. But then he's not of my generation either. He's twelve years younger." It's only fair to conclude that there are some egalitarian men out there. Vicky told us, "There are some very male men who are not wimps and who, in fact, are becoming pretty neat feminists. They're learning to look for the similarities and not put down the differences. I just haven't met them yet."

Kate's analysis of the New Man/New Woman partnership suggests that their relationship path may be strewn with mine fields, "I watch men struggling with women who are strong professionally, whose careers have outshone their husbands'. They've stayed married, but it has taken a lot of work on both sides. Sadly, these women often feel anguish about not being the wives and mothers they are expected to be. People say that a strong professional woman should never marry and have children because of the way she lives her life. Why shouldn't she expect to live the same way professional men have lived for centuries?"

One woman suggests that the emergence of the New Man may be hindered by women's difficulty in letting go of traditional roles, thus making it too easy for men to continue in their old ways, "Women of this generation haven't asked men to change. Women have done all the changing for them and tried to ease the transition. Some men will tell you that women aren't the way they used to be. They'll say, 'I think it's great what you gals are doing,' but in the end they still expect women to keep the home fires burning. Women have taken on too many roles and not asked men to share them. Women deal with change better—it's our natural state."

Yet, the emerging New Man may not be every New Woman's dream. According to Marjorie, "A brash, sexy European author wrote an article about how women talk a good game, but when they fall in love it isn't with liberated, feminist gentlemen. He wrote, 'These feminists are falling in love with men like me.' He made a very good point. What types of men are attractive to us and how do we relate to men who are really grappling with these issues? I personally don't find those men attractive, although they are my friends. Would I get involved in a relationship with one of them? No way. Why? I don't want to hear about or deal with their struggle."

New Truth: Hope for the future of relationships lies with women.

"I see great hope for relationships. We're between the stories of the history book. Nobody's telling us how to do it. We're reinventing relationships right now and it's very hard. I don't know one woman who has had an easy time. Or one man for that matter."

Torchbearers see hope for their relationships with men in the future, though not without caveats and reservations. "I have so much time invested in training this man that I'm not about to give up on him now," said one woman in a long-term marriage. Emily recognizes that the way to grow in life is through relationships with both men and women, "Men are changing, but extremely slowly. All we can do is be honest. If we happen to find a man, that's great. But it wouldn't be great unless we had our female friends to talk to. Deep relationships are with women. Surface relationships are with men." Rosa also expresses concern about the way her women friends are raising their sons, "I see hope for relationships, but not for changing the way certain roles are structured as long as these little boys aren't being taught to cook, make their beds, and do the laundry."

Several see women as the hope for building future relationships. "Men are just plowing around in the dark without a clue," says Annette. "They have been incredibly hurt and are very confused because they want a relationship just as much as women do. Men have been softened as a result of that pulverizing so they're more willing to be guided by women into new kinds of relationships. Relationships are changing, but the consequence for women has been exhaustion. At the same time, women have gained more of an understanding of strengths they didn't know they had." A similar perspective was offered by Georgia, who shares Annette's concern, "Male energy is needed for balance and for the survival of the planet. I'm asking for a miracle—that men's consciousness will change or women will so come into their power that men will recognize it and follow them."

"If you are a woman in this country who is our age, you've been given a great deal," one woman told us. "It's better for us than for guys our age." While it is true that women of the baby-boomer generation have been the recipients of many benefits, they've also given an enormous amount of attention and energy to creating unprecedented opportunities for the people they love to grow along with them. Nowhere is this more evident than in their efforts to build satisfying relationships with men. What emerges from their experiences with husbands, boyfriends, and male colleagues is that not only is there more work to be done, but that the future of male-female relationships rests in good (manicured) hands.

Chapter Eight

I'm Blessed to Have Women Friends Who are the Backbone of My Life

"Feminism has been a very convenient social movement for me because I always assumed that I could do whatever I wanted. It never occurred to me that being female would be a problem. I came of age at a time when this was just beginning to be possible. I didn't actually have a feminist revelation so much as it just fell the way I was going anyway."

Anita, fifty, is a successful artist. She moved to Mexico several years ago after a divorce and became involved in a passionate affair which ended badly. One night, she was feeling down and two of her girlfriends, both in their thirties, suggested a way for her to cheer up, "Why don't you go out to a bar and go dancing?" Anita told them, "I could never go to a bar by myself." Her friends didn't understand, "But you moved to a foreign country by yourself." Anita replied, "Sure, but I would never walk into a bar by myself."

Anita's logic makes perfect sense to the generation of women who have spent their entire lives being pushed in one direction by the restrictive rules of their girlhood and in the opposite way by the liberated precepts of their adulthood. Like many women of her generation, she carries baggage from the ultra-traditional 1950s that younger generations do not. In her mind, going to a bar alone is not a "nice girl" thing to do. Her younger girlfriends, who weren't raised on *Ozzie and Harriet* and *Donna Reed*, cannot understand this. But for Anita, the distinction is perfectly clear.

While second-wave feminism enabled women like Anita to break from conventional definitions of femininity and live a freer life, most women in this age group continue to struggle with the old messages and constraining social values of their mothers' generation. As a result, although they have benefited greatly—legally, professionally, and socially—from the efforts of the women's movement, many have trouble calling themselves feminists. In this chapter we explore three questions: 1) Do the women who benefited the most as a result of the women's movement identify themselves as feminists? 2) How have Torchbearers been impacted by the ultra-conservative femininity of the 1950s and the ultra-liberated feminism of the 1970s? 3) Is there any significant trend in the scope and nature of support systems for mid-life women, nearly to the point of a redefinition of the word "family"?

Do Torchbearers call themselves feminists?

"I look at younger women coming along in our wake and they seem to take it all for granted. They see the women's movement as something historical, like World War II."

In Wendy Wasserstein's play *American Daughter*, Lyssa Dent Hughes, a Zoe Baird-Kimba Woods-like character, has been nominated by the President of the United States to the Office of Surgeon General. The antithesis to baby-boomer Lyssa is Quincy, a younger political co-worker who gives little credit to the feminists who made her own career possible. Wasserstein views the character of Quincy with disapproval and disappointment. "It's one thing to encounter resistance to feminism, the word and the concept, from the generation ahead of you and quite another to see the generation behind you blithely dismissing the foundation that you've built your life upon," Wasserstein says.

New York Times journalist Sarah Boxer writes, "If time has won anything for feminism, it appears to be ingratitude." After examining nearly a dozen national polls conducted by newspapers and survey research firms, Boxer concludes that despite 75 percent of all women reporting that the status of their gender has improved in the last twenty-five years, few call themselves feminists. Boxer concludes that the problem lies with the terminology—the number of women who consider the label "feminist" an insult has increased over the last decade, while the number who think it is a compliment has been cut in half. Although some feel discomfort or a lack of identification with the women's movement, one would not expect this to be the case for women of this generation. To discover whether the women who profited first and foremost from second-wave feminism are proud to call themselves feminists, we asked each woman we interviewed, "Do you consider yourself a feminist? Why or why not?"

"I'm for equal rights but I'm not a feminist."

When we asked women if they considered themselves feminists, they answered, "That depends on how you define it," or "My definition of feminism may be different from yours." No one seems to know what the word means! Marilyn French defines feminism as "any attempt to improve conditions for any group of women through female solidarity and a female perspective." Barbara Ehrenrich writes that "feminism is a way of asking 'What's good for women?'" According to the dictionary, feminism is "a doctrine advocating social and political rights for women equal to those of men." Given these meanings, what contemporary woman of any age could *refuse* to call herself a feminist?

If the point of feminism was to win women a wider range of opportunities, then it has been incredibly successful. Yet, in the late 1990s, many women are reluctant to describe themselves as feminists or to even associate themselves with the women's movement. Various afflictions have been attributed to feminism including everything from the man shortage to the infertility epidemic to female burnout. Beginning in the early 1980s, the press, the advertising industry, the religious Right, conservative politicians, and the entertainment industry began to convey the impression that the women's movement was obsolete. Today, people shy away from the word "feminist" despite the fact that the majority of adult females believe the women's movement has improved their lives. Many women believe the women's movement still hasn't gone far enough.

Considering the power and the solidarity of the forces directed against feminism, its success in improving women's lives in so brief a time is astounding. Through feminism, girls who were taught that their only goals in life were to become wives and mothers, learned to look beyond these aspirations and embrace a wider world. But there are those who feel this has been a bittersweet victory. Women of this generation, while in many ways the prime beneficiary of feminism, may also be in the age group most affected by its failures. Many women thought that once they were "liberated" from conventional expectations, men and women would both have careers and home lives with each partner carrying an equal load. But women found they couldn't have it all. As comic Steven Wright explains, "You can't have it all. Where would you put it?"

New Truth: You must live your feminism.

> "When I became a sports writer, I was plunged into a new world. There were no other women at work. I was always being ragged on by men. At first, I was very insecure, but I stayed strong. I blazed the trail into the locker room trying to gain equal access. I had to live my feminism."

Feminists have been accused of many things: They don't care about families. They are strident and angry, particularly at men. They are unfeminine. They are against marriage and motherhood. They are radical, bra-burning, political activists who spend their time meeting in groups and reading women's literature. No wonder so many women hesitate to use the term.

Amazingly, fewer than half the women we interviewed respond with an irrefutable "yes" when asked if they consider themselves feminists. Of those who say "yes," many couch their answers in rhetoric that conveys that they are middle-of-the-road feminists, not one of those "other kinds." Few women answer as strongly as this forty-four-year-old mother of three daughters, "I am very much a feminist in every possible way. I feel a responsibility to other women and to my daughters. How many ways can you be a feminist? I am a feminist in all those ways." More typical is the woman who told us, "As far as equal pay for equal jobs, comparable educational opportunities, women having a right to say what's on their minds, a right to do with their bodies as they please, then yes, I am 100 percent feminist in those areas. But I also like guys doing things for me. I like doors opened. I like chairs pulled out. I like flowers." When did "feminists are against flowers" get added to the laundry list of accusations?

> *"It's only when I'm up against the cultural heat that denies women's rights or when society forces me to take a stand that I feel the need to announce that I'm a feminist."*

For every woman who distances herself from the word, many speak passionately about why they are proud to call themselves feminists. In the last few years, Torchbearers are reminded once again, why the women's movement must continue to be viable as they witness the fate of their peers Anita Hill, Lani Guinier, and Hillary Rodham Clinton. Jerri, a forty-four-year-old lawyer, feels her connection to feminism has deepened over the years. "It took me a while to warm up to that word or idea. Like a lot of women, I used to say, 'I'm for equal rights but I'm not a feminist.' Now I feel strongly committed to the feminist movement.

As we move into power positions, the more threatened the established order is. During the Clarence Thomas Supreme Court confirmation hearings, all the women in my office stopped working for three days. We sat around the television set screaming and throwing things. That crystallized a lot of my thinking about feminism and how hard it is to be a woman. The Anita Hill episode makes it clear that we still have to work together and point out sexist things when they happen."

Susan Faludi's *Backlash* brought a powerful message to millions of women whose career success lulled them into thinking that perhaps there was no further need for a women's movement. Sarah says, "I read *Backlash* not too long ago and I sat there pounding my fist with every sentence, saying, 'Yes! Yes! When will we wake up and do something about this?'" Deena offers her response, "I had a very severe and intimate reaction to this book. I was constantly putting the book down to digest sections of it because so much anger came up for me. On the one hand, we have made great gains, but in reality we have barely taken two baby steps towards equality. I have a deep concern that we're backsliding. I don't want to see that happen."

"I've called myself a feminist for years. I have to be."

Beth, a labor organizer and mother of two, has no ambivalence about calling herself a feminist but understands why some have trouble with the word. "I have some friends who interpret feminism in the narrowest sense," she says. "When I got married, some of my women friends were very unhappy with my choice. When I had marital problems, they were very supportive of my leaving my husband! That is oppressive and unfeminist. As opposed to seeing any value in my struggle, or being in the struggle with me, most of them had a very strong point of view. I consider myself a militant feminist. Being a feminist has been a critical part of my identity since my twenties. I have never questioned its significance in my life. As a union organizer, I work hard on projects I consider critical for women. I've tried to insert those issues into the contract language, whether it is the right to have family leave, medical care for dependents, on-site child care, flexible shifts, the ability to work part-time, or educational opportunities for women related to career advancement. These are all feminist issues."

Unlike Beth, many women take great pains to identify themselves as social, rather than political, feminists. Although a guiding principle of the women's movement stated that the personal *is* political, we often heard: "I see feminism as an intellectual and emotional opportunity to relate to people as people." "I'm more of a humanist or an individualist." "I prefer the word womanist." "I'm not politically motivated. I'm motivated for the spiritual empowerment of women." Womanist. Humanist. Individualist. Spritualist. Equalist. Any "ist" but feminist.

"I never considered myself a feminist. That word is too strong-sounding. I stand behind women's issues and women's rights. I'm very much in favor of women having an equal place in society and the workplace. I believe in most of the things that feminism represents, but I've never believed in a radical approach."

A surprising number of women talk the talk but won't walk the walk. We often heard, "I'm a feminist in every sense of the word, yet, I'd never call myself one." Edna realizes that she would not be working as a building contractor, a previously male-dominated profession, if not for the niche feminism has carved for women like her. Nonetheless, she told us, "I wouldn't call myself a feminist, but I'm glad to reap all the benefits."

Even more puzzling is the response from Susannah who is the primary breadwinner in her family. "I would never use the word 'feminist,'" she says. "If you told me what the word means, I might be every single one of those things. I kept my last name. I am a professional working woman. I earn three times what my husband makes. I believe that women should have equal opportunity to participate in all phases of life and engage as equal partners in whatever endeavors they choose to undertake. I am for women having opportunities outside the home. I am conscious and aware of women's rights, but I wouldn't call myself a feminist."

"Gloria Steinem has never been my role model."

For the generation of women who spent the first fifteen to twenty years of their life wanting to be Doris Day and the next twenty wanting to be Gloria Steinem, there will never be total ease with terms like "women's rights," "female solidarity," or "feminist agenda." But some women seem to be in total denial. Elaine owns a highly successful catering company. She told us, "I have never considered myself a feminist. I've never felt I couldn't do things because I'm a woman. I've never felt locked out. I've always believed if you want to do something, if you're a man or a woman, you just figure it out and do it."

Clearly, for some, even the idea of feminism pushes a lot of buttons. A few women claim never to have experienced gender bias or to have been sexually harassed or subjected to insensitive and inappropriate comments from male colleagues. And yes, these women have worked full-time in professional positions for over twenty years. Nancy, forty, CEO of a large software company, claims not to be a feminist at all. "Feminism has been very harmful to men and women's relationships. I like men to be men. My girlfriends get angry when I say that. They ask me if I really would want to live the way my mother did in the '50s. I tell them, 'That wouldn't have happened to me.' I have been in the workplace for twenty years working primarily with men. I have never been sexually harassed. When I walk into a business meeting, men notice me because I'm attractive. Some guy might say, 'That's an attractive dress you're wearing,' or 'Did you do something different with your hair?' Another women might say this is sexual harassment but I love it. I'll say, 'Thank you. It's so nice that you noticed.' I'm not suggesting that he ask me out or follow up with anything else. I just give him what he wants— some attention. I'm very anti-feminist." It seems Nancy has added "feminists don't like compliments" to the list of bad traits associated with feminism.

> *"In the middle of my career, I thought that you get where you are because of your abilities. Maybe it's not so male-dominated—quit complaining and get out there. Now that I'm in management and find myself working at a different*

level with men, I'm a little more radical and a little more angry. I realize things haven't changed much. I was just out of it for a while."

Some women have always been feminists, some women have never been feminists, and some women were feminists at one time and aren't now or vice versa. With the passage of time, the children of feminists will possibly be so egalitarian that the debate over whether one is or is not a feminist hopefully will be unnecessary. As Lili told us, "About ten years ago, I went public as a feminist. I was fooled for a while thinking that by working under the table that I was out of the system and had control over my life. That was an illusion. It was much more empowering to step forward publicly as a feminist. One of the lowest moments came in the 1980s when feminism was a dirty word. That was a very trying time. I talked to men and women and had many dialogues and arguments about what it means to be a feminist. I'm hopeful that it will be accepted again." Perhaps, in the end, whether a woman calls herself a feminist may not really matter. As one woman puts it, "Is it more important that I claim to be a feminist or that I just go out there and act like one?"

How do Torchbearers cope with 1950s femininity and 1970s feminism?

"I have to be careful not to get caught up in what I'm supposed to do, as opposed to what I want to do."

The women of the baby-boom generation feel the push and pull of two competing ideologies—the one they grew up with which told them to be good girls, nurture people, obey rules, not be aggressive, and put others first. Those childhood precepts became outdated when they entered adolescence and young womanhood in the heyday of women's liberation. Later, women were told they could be assertive, independent, successful, and put their own needs at an equal level with others. Many people feel that the challenge of this generation, and what makes them so interesting, is having to integrate those two diametric points of view.

All their lives, women of this generation have heard mixed messages. It's the contradiction of "Stand by your man" versus "Have a career." As one woman told us, "I feel like I've got earphones on and each ear piece has a different message coming through. I'm trying to hear two different messages at once." Most Torchbearers were raised with a rigid set of expectations for female behavior. One woman recalls the horror of having to wear a girdle at age fourteen. "I had no hips. I had no shape. I didn't know why I was wearing a girdle, but God forbid you should jiggle, even if there was nothing to jiggle. Girdles are a metaphor for how constricting and narrow those years were." Now, even though we recognize that era as extreme and unnatural in its glorification of ultra-domesticity, women still hear voices—from church, from guidance counselors, from anyone who ever told them no. Kim, an artist, told us, "All my friends hear these little voices in our ears all the time. We try not to be imprisoned by them."

There are two perspectives about the experiences of the baby-boom generation. One is that their need to accommodate two antithetical models of womanhood—feminism and femininity—has made them schizophrenic. The other is that this is a very fortunate generation to have been born when they were. At the conclusion of each interview, we asked, "Unlike women in their twenties and early thirties, women of your generation carry the baggage of the pre-liberation era. In other words, there are two competing models for women your age, the traditional model of the 1950s and the feminist model of the 1970s. In what ways do these models manifest themselves in your life?"

Many described their lives as a balancing act: "I'm a paradox. I'm living multiple existences that are barely on the same wave length." "I am climbing a rock wall every single step of the way." "I'm in-between chapters." "I walk a fine line." "I have a foot in both camps."

Meg is currently a legislative analyst, but throughout most of the 1970s she was a flower child. Despite her professional success, she continues to feel torn between continuing her current lifestyle or adopting a more nontraditional way of living. "On the one hand, I'm just like my dad, trapped in his suburban life. I've got the mortgage, the car, and the mutual funds. I hear his voice saying, 'Meg, if you keep saving and investing your money, you're going to be able to retire a wealthy woman.' So I hang in there. I have a personal trainer. I take nice vacations, but I'm pulled the other way all the time. It's a constant fight. Every day, when I get off the bus and walk into my office building, I'm thinking, 'Maybe today is the day I'm going to stop, put on my hippie clothes, and go dance in the field.' "

"Anytime the pendulum swings radically in one direction, and I think that is what happened in the '60s, someone ends up having to pay the price."

When you ask women about how they manage competing roles and expectations, you often hear about housekeeping, laundry, cooking, child care, and the holidays. Women of this generation are constantly second guessing themselves about what they, as the standard of all nurturing behavior, should be doing. Carole, a paralegal with three children, recalls, "I thought I couldn't be a good mother if I didn't bake all the birthday cakes and sew all the Halloween costumes." Jane, an accountant, has been married for over twenty years. "I feel liberated, but every so often I see myself slipping. I find myself doing something because it is expected of me, like sending out Christmas cards or making cakes from scratch. If I step back and ask myself, 'Why am I doing this?' the answer is that it's something my mother did. Little things creep out from my traditional background. I call it my baggage."

Patricia, a fashion designer, compares her frenetic pace to being the "slow man trying to catch up." She claims to be worn out by taking on new roles, yet she never has let go of the old ones. Patricia carries on certain traditions for her daughter because she feels children want to know there are rituals in their life. "Take, for example, the traditional Christmas thing. I have watched so many women fall apart, myself included, and I've done it for several years. You're trying to create a perfect holiday and a sense of domesticity—the beautiful tree, the presents, the family dinner, the whole thing. This year, Christmas was the worst disaster I've ever had. I stopped functioning because I realized that I was trying to present a picture that's not real."

If there is one emotion most Torchbearers share it is guilt. Caryl, an ESL instructor at a community college, knows her husband is proud of her and does not expect her to serve in a traditional role. Nonetheless, she puts that expectation on herself. "The competing messages are there. I used to feel guilty as hell about having a house cleaner, but I don't any more. In fact, I want it once a week instead of once every two weeks." Kathleen, a human resources manager, thought she had rejected the traditional model until her children were born. Then she says she turned right around and embraced it. "I never stop feeling conflicted about whether I give enough time to my children. When I take time for my family, something slips in my career. My husband probably suffers the most because he's the one who is always the third party. He doesn't deserve that."

As a generation of "good girls," many feel they have to be perfect. Diane, a marketing director for a large computer company, wants to do a good job at whatever she does. She admits to perfectionism. "I grew up in the purest, most unadulterated structure—a Catholic female upbringing. I remember going to politeness classes where they taught us how to eat potato chips with a spoon. I was conditioned for a life which I am not living." Julie, a new bride and new mom, is also a busy executive recruiter. She married for the first time at forty and wants to be a perfect wife. "My husband will ask me to do something that's related to his business and I think, 'I have my own business. I have things I need to tend to.' Then I'll step back and say, 'Am I being a good wife? Am I being supportive? Maybe I should have done what he needed me to do.'" Jill, a physician, grew up in a large family. As the oldest, she learned how to cook pastas and cannoli from scratch when she was five years old. Jill admits that her need to be meticulous about everything drove those around her crazy. "I was a fanatic about being neat. I was compulsive about never running out of milk or eggs at home. Then my career got busy, I had a son, and I couldn't figure out how to do everything. Being perfect became a non-issue."

> *"The blending of the feminist and the feminine, the left brain and the right brain, the old and new has enabled us to move forward and bring the best of each of those ideologies into an integrated self."*

Society depends on stereotypes to categorize people, limit them, and isolate them. Kelly, the director of a home health agency, told us that she used to be embarrassed to say she was a nurse because people would see her as a traditional woman. Although it is a struggle, most women of this generation reject labels and being pigeon-holed into either-or roles. Marie, a small business owner and mother of one son, is incensed about the Mommy Track versus the Career Track debate. "It makes women feel inadequate. Women who choose one or the other aren't judgmental about women who don't make the same choices. If three women sat down together, one who has a career, one who is at home raising a family, and one who is doing both, they wouldn't be naturally antagonistic. Instead, they would talk about the issues they have in common. Now, we all feel inadequate and that wasn't anyone's intention. The pendulum unfortunately has to swing farther than you want in order to make a point. Women need to support each other more than ever, because they're doing a damn good job." Pam speaks for many women by rejecting the idea that she has to choose between being either feminine or feminist. "I stumble along, make it up as I go, and do the best I can. Katherine Hepburn is my hero—she didn't worry about how she was labeled. She was a pioneer. I admire somebody who disregards labels, rules, and roles, and does what she wants."

Baby-boomer women are the ultimate "good girls." If they have a generational flaw, it is a tendency to do too much. Rita, a hotel executive, is convinced that this generation of women doesn't know how to ask for help. "Asking for help is probably the last thing that most of us think about. We care for our babies and yet feel guilty that we're not at work. At work, we feel guilty that we aren't caring for our babies. The Civil War rages in all our minds."

Because of the way they saw their mothers behave at home, many women cannot shake off the need to do everything, even when their spouse does not expect or demand traditional female behavior. Amanda married for the first time at thirty-eight. Prior to her marriage, she rented a business office in a small industrial park. After her marriage, she moved her work to a spare bedroom at home because she felt this was the best way to be a wife. "I feel I must make dinner every night. When my husband comes home from work, I have dinner ready. I make sure the house is clean. I do the domestic chores. I will frequently work at my desk until it's time to start dinner, go start dinner, go back to work at my desk, work until my husband gets home, make and serve dinner, do the dishes, then go back and finish working. My husband told me when we were dating that he did not marry me to cook his dinners, take his clothes to the cleaners, and clean his house. Those were things he could hire somebody to do. He wanted me as his companion, as the person he shared his time with. Even though he has told me that very clearly, I still feel it's my job."

New Truth: Create balance in your life.

Sylvia Hewlett, author of *A Lesser Life*, writes about the "double burden of gratuitous psychological pressures" placed on women based on wildly inflated notions of 1950s femininity. The women we interviewed were caught between the '50s cult of motherhood and contemporary feminism. Hewlett writes, "An American woman trying to fulfill the demands of both traditions is obviously in something of a dilemma. It is not easy to be simultaneously the earth mother-goddess and the hard-bitten, hard-nosed corporate executive or fire person. And her attempt to manage both roles is further undermined by the fact that American society, having produced the strongest and most anti-thetical dual roles for women, has left them with the weakest support systems with which to mediate these roles."

In the 1990s, however, imagining life without feminism is difficult to do. Many changes begun in the late '60s and early '70s are now an integral part of daily existence. Only in the last thirty years have women gained legal and reproductive rights, pursued higher education, entered the professions, and over-turned antiquated beliefs about social roles. Women's achieve-ments are now presumed. Marilyn French identifies the subtle, and not so subtle, ways that have been used to defeat feminism and return women to their previous status: "Rescind its victories (ban abortion); confine women to lower employment levels (glass ceiling); found movements aimed at returning women to subordinate status (fundamentalism)." Most Torchbearers are grateful to the women's movement for providing a mechanism which allowed them to break from conventional definitions of femininity in order to pursue a more autonomous life.

The challenge for all women is to strike a balance between their true feminine nature and their need to be competent and productive workers, without guilt or labels and without being reluctant to ask for help when needed. Connie married for the first time at age forty. She is also president of her own company. "Having balance makes you a total person," she told us. "I have a nice balance of femininity and independence. If I'm in a situation where it's in my best interest to be more feminine, I don't look at that as being bad. I'm not stuck in one role or the other. Some women are stuck in the feminist role or never got out of the feminine one. They don't realize they are just playing a role."

How do Torchbearers view their women friends?

"Women need to help other women. It would be a blessing if more women had an understanding of what we've lived through in this generation because it's been very, very tough."

Cybil Shepherd, actress and singer, says of all the songs on her recent CD, the one about friendship is her favorite. The song honors her women friends who were with her through thick and thin, during and in-between marriages, before and after children, and in good times and bad. Despite the confusion some women of this generation have about feminism or their on-going struggle with femininity and liberation, one fact is certain: they love their women friends and rely on them greatly. Because they have different kinds of personal connections and commitments from previous generations, their definition of family has expanded to include mutually supportive relationships with women friends and colleagues. Why, we wondered, have women friends become so important and integral in the lives of mid-life women?

Towards the end of each interview, we asked each woman, "Women of our generation have different kinds of connections and interdependencies and commitments from previous generations. Who is your family now?"

Many Torchbearers continue to be close to their parents and siblings, as well as the men in their lives, often referring to their husband or partner as their best friend. But surprisingly often, they count their friendships with women as most significant. Claire, an only child, feels lucky to have supportive friends whose love and comfort enabled her to survive the devastating loss of her mother. "When my mother died, my mother's mother decided that she didn't want anything to do with me or my father so we were totally isolated from the immediate family. That first Christmas it was my dad and me in a hotel in Palm Springs. What pulled me through were two close girlfriends calling me everyday and asking, 'Are you OK?' and knowing that I could pick up the phone at any time, day or night, and talk to them. They mean more to me than a family because I have chosen to have them in my life."

"We are products of a generation of consciousness raising."

Females of all ages have always relied on other women, but the deep trust, openness, and self-revelatory nature of conversations between women friends is a contemporary phenomenon which has its roots in the consciousness raising (CR) movement of the late 1960s. For many women who were taking their first tentative steps towards new ways of thinking and acting, membership in a CR group was a seminal event. Gloria was in a women's group that remained together for most of the 1970s. "I had a wonderful experience with my CR group," she told us. "We are talking about a reunion now because everyone's life was changed by being a part of that group. There were moments in my life when, if I hadn't been in that group, I would have decompensated. It was the first time that we could really talk for a long time, be listened to, and not feel judged. When we thought we were saying something really stupid, really private, or really nasty, two or three other women would say, 'I feel exactly the same way.' That was very affirming, empowering, and unique to that time. There was new pride in being a woman. I'm not sure that women's groups would catch on right now, but it was important in the '70s because we were really hungry for it."

For many, the women's movement and CR shared a common goal—liberating women in a sexist culture. For some, CR was political; for others it was not. Rebecca, a college professor, recalls her own experience in the mid-'70s with a group of women graduate students who met every week for three years. At the time, she was married to a man who was openly unfaithful and often absent, despite the serious illness of one of their daughters. "I became very close to the women who were in my CR group. It was the most organized period of intellectual and emotional growth for me in terms of getting to know who I was. It wasn't a fad or a superficial experience. It was very deep communication. I wouldn't have had the strength to make the decision to divorce my husband before I was in the group."

Barbara Ehrenrich writes that "feminism raised women's conversational expectations—they discovered the possibilities of conversation as an act of collective creativity; the intimate sharing of personal experience, the weaving of the personal into the general and the political, the adventure of freewheeling speculation unrestrained by boundaries." Marti, a chemist, told us that her women's group has been together for nineteen years, although only five out of the twelve original members meet regularly. "We've been through so much," Marti told us. "Every life issue, every life cycle you can think of has happened within this group from birth to death and everything in between. It's a real family that gives all of us a grounding. There is such a bond. I know I could depend on them if I needed to—and I have. It's great to be able to sit there and not say anything, just to be somewhere I belong."

New Truth: You've got to have friends.

"I talk everything through with my girlfriends. I have different girlfriends for different issues."

With today's mobile society, families are separated geographically and adult children live hundreds and even thousands of miles from where they were born. For some, the physical distance is as great as the psychological distance. Betty, an architect from the East Coast who now lives in Colorado, describes the gulf between herself and her mother and siblings as "immeasurable. I can't even begin to tell you how much of a chasm there is between the way I view my life and the way they view my life. So I've had to restructure my definition of family."

Due to geographic mobility, career and family responsibilities, and different lifestyle choices, female friendships have supplanted the biological family. Sadly, many Torchbearers feel their parents and other relatives know very little about the interesting adult women they have become. Kerry, a banker, told us, "My family is not very close. We see each other every seventeen years whether we need to or not."

Conversely, they have wonderful things to say about their friendships with women:

> *"Women are the ones I call on to laugh with, to get support from, and to touch base and connect with."*

> *"I depend on my girlfriends greatly for reinforcement, reassurance, and support. Even for a 'Hey, how ya' doin'?— Great, how are you?' It's reinforcing just to hear their voices and have someone who understands."*

> *"I can turn to them when I'm sick. I can turn to them for financial help. I can turn to them for emotional support at any time, day or night."*

As women of this generation age and begin to think about life after retirement, they inevitably think about the community of women friends they hope to grow old with. Susan, only forty-four, anticipates the day when she and her friends will be old. Susan and six other women have co-purchased a home to be used now for summer vacations and, in the future, as a permanent or semi-permanent home for their later years. "We call ourselves the Ladies of the Lake. We used to go to the lake with our families when we were little kids. Now we are in our late forties and we still go there together every year. We're an odd kind of group but we're still connected after all these years. When we get together, we put on old records and dance to the same songs we danced to when we were fourteen years old. We look at each other, aging and spreading out, and we joke about putting in a wheelchair ramp and wondering whose chair will be the first empty one at the table.

"When I'm with them I can be a kid again and act like I don't have all these responsibilities. Yet, I also see that I'm maturing, getting smarter, and taking better care of myself. I'll always have them. Whoever is left of us, we'll roll up the wheelchair ramp and dance. I like the idea of ending up like that—in a community of people like myself, my extended family."

Chapter Nine

I Tell Women to Keep Walking and Remember to Pass the Torch

"It's tough being a role model, especially when you don't know where you're going."

As a generation, baby-boomer women fashioned entirely new ways for adult women to live, love, and work, yet they rarely think of themselves as pioneers. Lisa is the only female senior vice-president at a large multinational bank and, at age forty-three, a first-time mom. Would she call herself a pioneer? "I don't think so," Lisa says. "I certainly chose to enter a profession that has been less traveled by women, and I had a baby late in life without a husband or partner which was unheard of when I was a girl, but am I a pioneer? I wouldn't give myself that status." If women like Lisa do not credit themselves as being pacesetters, how do they explain their risk-taking behaviors and their dogged willingness to confront impossible challenges?

In the second part of the interview, we asked participants to look beyond their personal experiences and comment on some larger issues which shed light on their uniqueness as a generation. In contrast to earlier questions which focused on specific stages of development in their own lives, this required some self-reflection in order to step back and look at their female peers through a broader lens. We asked four key questions related to the absence of rules, seeing oneself as a pioneer, advice for younger women, and planning for the future.

"In the absence of rules or role models, it was not possible to follow the path of a previous generation. How has this affected women of your age?"

"There were no rules, so experimentation was almost a given. The free wheeling, sexual revolution, consciousness raising, let's-give-it-a-try-and-see-if-it-flies atmosphere, allowed us to really go places and do things that were never available before."

The women of this generation have been remarkably resourceful and adaptable. Although they entered young adulthood without clear guidelines, rules, or role models, they somehow succeeded in arenas where few women had gone before. There are two discrepant views of the period of social upheaval that began in the late 1960s and early 1970s. Those with a positive view hearken back to those years as a time of choice, opportunity, and unprecedented freedom. Others recall that era as confusing, difficult, and full of trial and error. As one woman told us, "I had answers when I was a kid. Now I'm not even sure what the questions are." Torchbearers are of two minds about what it's been like to live through a time in history when the old order was challenged and new ways were being invented on a daily basis. For most, it has been a period of unprecedented freedom; for some it has been perplexing and intimidating. Bonnie is a volunteer with recent Russian immigrants. She sees a parallel between their lives and her own peers. "Our generation is in a really unique position. We had many opportunities, but nothing prepared us to take advantage of them. I work with immigrants who come from a culture in which there are limited options. When they got to this country, they didn't know what to do with themselves. Their teenagers are going wild because they have all this freedom for the first time. It's analogous to what happened to us."

Those we interviewed were raised to "behave a certain way." They were not prepared to face choices about whether or not to have children, whether they could have both a full career and a family, or whether they could have children and no partner. Consequently, decisions were often made on-the-fly without considering the consequences. Marsha, a dentist, feels she and her friends stumbled along making decisions when previously they didn't even have choices. "We fell down a lot because we didn't have wise counsel from our mothers to say, 'Honey, here's what I did when I was your age,' or 'What can I do that would give you some platform to stand on?' It was like trying to walk on quicksand. And when we sank, we sank clear up to our necks before we asked for help. We were choking and spitting out sand before we finally said, 'I'm not doing very well.'"

Harriet was an outstanding student and an obedient, compliant daughter until she dropped out of college in 1969 to live in a commune. "From the day I was born through high school, there were very clear absolutes which I obeyed," Harriet recalls. "My first year in college, my life went from everything being black and white to shades of gray, which was shocking and unsettling. My boyfriend won my heart by saying, 'There is no such thing as right and wrong, good and bad,' which was a totally new idea to me. He meant that everything was tainted with some of both and that blew my mind."

Like Harriet, Evelyn was also dazzled by the rapid changes occurring in the late 1960s. "My senior year in high school was the craziest time," Evelyn remembers. "Suddenly, there were all these possibilities opening for girls who had been raised with so much social and behavioral control. Those who saw these choices as opportunities, who could let go of the shackles they had grown up with, are the pioneers of our times. But having choices brings about more confusion, especially if you haven't been educated to make decisions on your own. If you've learned self-determination along the way, and if you have the tools to evaluate the consequences, then having choices is a joy."

Almost 50 percent of those we interviewed used the word "confusing" to describe the impact of coming of age during a social and cultural revolution. Mary was raised in a Cantonese-speaking household by standards that can only be described as extremely traditional. At eighteen, she married an older man selected by her family. Ten years later, she left the marriage despite her parents' objections. "Because of the way I was raised, I was supposed to live a certain way which was in conflict with what was inside me, what I wanted to do, and what I had the capability to do. I ultimately left my marriage because I couldn't play a false role anymore," she says.

Even today, women in their forties and fifties feel the residual effect of not being prepared as girls for the adult world they have had to live in. Barbara, a software developer, feels that this has left her generation with the sense of not knowing what they're supposed to be doing. "There's a part of us that can sometimes just go a little nuts. Given the combination of self-doubt and exhilaration, we didn't know if we were liberated or not. In 1971, I wrote a paper with the title 'I Let You Be Liberated,' which was something my then-husband actually said to me! We've really gone through it. Were we fish? Were we fowl? Some of us still don't know."

New Truth: Take chances. Be feminist enough to know you should.

If the absence of rules has been a source of confusion, it has also been a source of strength. "It was enlightening for us to learn that there were alternatives," Maria, a college professor, says. "Today, we have more women in leadership positions, more women willing to take chances, and more women who are constantly moving toward realizing their dreams. There has been a removal of the fear that women are supposed to hold back their inner drive. When we reach out for something and are successful, this gives us the incentive to continue reaching out for something else. What we have done is so valuable for women who are twenty to thirty years younger. They take having alternatives as a matter of course, whereas we never could." Janet, a graduate student, agrees, "Opportunities were there for us and when we took advantage of them without major repercussions, we were able to move forward more confidently. Our peers were very instrumental to what was happening. If we didn't get encouragement at home, we could get it from other women because they were out there with us. We were changing the world together. My peer group, by giving me license to explore and grow, has been very instrumental in allowing me to become who I am."

Many women believe that the absence of rules had a mostly positive effect on their generation. Kathy, a book editor, believes that "women learned to utilize talents and skills they might not otherwise have been able to. If there is a negative aspect, it's that while we got to try new things, we still had the old ones to do as well." Margaret, an artist, is pleased that there was a point in history which ushered in an era of personal growth without boundaries, "I had to establish a code of ethics for myself. I had to decide what my limits were. I had to decide how far I was willing to go with some risky behaviors. As a result, I came into my own. I became independent and started making decisions from the inside out, instead of from the outside in." These women are proud of themselves and their peers for taking risks. Most agree that while it's harder to make up the rules yourself, it can also be more satisfying.

New Truth: If it's trial by fire, don't forget to bring along some marshmallows.

In the late '60s and early '70s, experimentation was expected. Some women believed that if they created something new and different, it would be struggle-free. But the rejection of old rules and the opportunity to shape new ones did not come without adversity. As one woman told us, "A lot of rules were removed, but it was difficult to completely break out. The old ways were so ingrained in terms of how to respond and react that it was a difficult adjustment." The effort to become *somebody* did not come about without heartache or sacrifice. Robin, a non-practicing attorney, says, "It's been traumatic. It's been exhausting. We felt alone. We felt misunderstood. We felt torn. But we couldn't go back."

Because they have a greater number of opportunities than previous generations of women, some feel guilty if they are not accomplishing more. As one woman told us, "If I'm not a judge or a best-selling author or a doctor, then I feel like there's something wrong with me. I should be at the top, the brightest of everything. For those of us who once wanted to be the best teachers or the best nurses, it's a totally different game. There's a feeling of wanting to do it all and then sensing that I'm not doing enough. I have a chance to become a hero and make a mark, but it's also a setup for failure if what I try to do doesn't work. I have the opportunity to be unique, to do something, be noticed, and lead the way. At the same time, I could shoot myself in the foot."

New Truth: Take the hero's journey.

Although baby-boomer women had liberties previous generations did not, Roberta, a college instructor, believes progress has been impeded because they are constantly encountering unfamiliar situations. "We don't move forward easily. When we take a step, we sometimes walk off the edge of the cliff. So we crawl back up, go ten more steps down the road, and there's another cliff. My generation has had to master the hero's journey. In that myth, the hero has to lose what she's had and then go through the process of self-discovery in order to continue her travels and reach a better place. We miss out if we're not willing to take the hero's journey."

While some feel that having to rewrite the rule book has been scary, traumatic, and exhausting, there is no desire to reinstate the rules they grew up with. As one woman told us, "If we want the old rules, we have to accept the boundaries that go with them." Jane, a militant activist in the 1960s and a professional chef today, says, "I run across a lot of powerful women who weren't around in such great numbers twenty-five years ago. The Vietnam War, feminism, and the civil rights movement were the catalysts that opened our eyes, enabled us to act as equals to men, and reach the levels of achievement we always should have had. The flood gates opened and the walls came down as to what women could and could not do. As a result, the world will never be the same."

"Would you describe yourself as a pioneer?"

"Maybe I'm a pioneer but I don't see anybody following me. I've had such a hard time cutting down the trees in front of me that I haven't looked behind to see if my life has influenced anyone else's. My family and friends see me as a pioneer, but it's hard to see one's self in that role."

If Torchbearers see themselves as pioneers at all, it is because they discern that they have behaved differently from previous generations. They also acknowledge that they have been trailblazers—some would say guinea pigs—in the world of work.

Overall, they feel the word "pioneer" implies that they intentionally initiated things which they mistakenly believe transpired by accident or happenstance. In retrospect, most agree they should take some credit, both individually and as a generation, for being pacesetters.

Some of those we interviewed could not connect themselves with the idea of being an innovator and said, flat-out, "Not me. I don't consider myself a pioneer." Annie, an accountant, says she doesn't see pioneering as part of her personality, while Ellen, a talented musician, views her abilities as gifts which she simply used as expected. Sheer modesty, not feeling that they had the courage to be first, or crediting the women who went before them are some reasons why women of this generation eschew pioneer status for themselves. Carolyn, a businesswoman, says, "People like Betty Friedan and Gloria Steinem are the real pioneers, although in my own quiet way, I rejected powerful social expectations well before that was the thing to do." There are many unstated reasons why these women are "reluctant pioneers." They were raised in a climate of "be seen and not heard" and "don't blow your own horn." Given the powerful "should" messages of their childhood that they clearly violated or rejected in adulthood, some have difficulty acknowledging that they are worthy of that appellation.

Mary Jo grapples with the issue of whether she is a pioneer because she just did what needed to be done. "A pioneer is someone who leads the way and I'm not sure I did that. I didn't follow a conventional way. I took on professional responsibilities very early. I changed careers several times. I went against my family's wishes when I married. Maybe accepting my own choices as being OK could be seen as pioneering, but there are so many people today who have taken risks and done things differently that maybe we are all pioneers. I asked my grandmother, who immigrated to this country from Ireland, how she was able to do that. She said, 'If I had been the only one, then that would have been special. But there were lots of us so we were all in it together.' When I step back, I can say, 'Perhaps my friends and I are pioneers but, within the context of our lives, it feels pretty ordinary.'"

New Truth: Be a personal pioneer.

If the women of this generation give themselves any recognition as being pioneers, it would be in the area of personal development. Although Cathy is highly successful as a government policy analyst and consultant in the computer industry, what she values most is her own personal growth. "The most courageous thing I've ever done is to pursue my inner work. There's nothing I'm more proud of. I pioneered new territory by exploring my own pain and anger and I am telling you, it was worth it."

Joan, a writer and single-parent, sees herself as a pioneer because she lives according to what her heart and spirit tell her is right for herself and her son. "Pioneers remake their circumstances," she says. "They transcend from one state to another because they want things to be better, even if they risk getting scalped in the middle of some dusty plain. Pioneers believe that things will turn out better for having made difficult choices. I've moved beyond the limitations of my upbringing by picking up the threads of my life and weaving them into something of real value. Everything I've done has contributed to my enrichment and growth as a person and as a parent to my son. I'm a pioneer in how I've structured my family because none of the things I do to raise him—things that I believe are spiritually, morally, and intellectually right—were ever done for me."

Breaking new ground is another aspect of personal pioneering. Going back to school as an adult, starting a new career, running a company in a male-dominated industry, holding "first woman" positions in various industries, shifting from a career viewed as "traditionally female" to one viewed as "traditionally male," and starting support organizations for women in the workplace were viewed as personal accomplishments that also impact the lives of others.

For Elaine, pioneering involves "self motivation, constantly being able to establish real internal values without having to depend on the reflection society or others give back to you. This requires making hard personal choices, where previously there were no guidelines." In college, Elaine challenged discriminatory rules and restrictions, initially fighting against curfews and dress codes, and later in young adulthood, marching for equal rights for women. Now in her forties, she recently walked away from success by selling her business and returning to graduate school for a degree in theology.

Being "among the first" is part of Jeanette's definition of a pioneer. She was not only the first in her family to go to college but to earn a doctorate as well. As an African-American, she grew up in an oppressive and segregated environment. Pioneering, for her, involves working every day to build humane and open-minded relationships with people from all racial, religious, and ethnic groups. For both Elaine and Jeanette, their individual life choices provide the basis for calling themselves pioneers.

New Truth: Take credit for the seeds that you've planted.

Nancy, the vice president of a commercial real estate firm, says, "I never thought of myself as a pioneer. I thought of myself as just selling a product, but many younger women whom I mentor consider me a pioneer. In my profession, the amount of money you make determines how you are valued. When I went on commission, the vice president of the company told me, 'Most women aren't successful in this field,' so I worked all the time. I was the first woman in the company to close over a million dollars in one month, but in my mind, I was thinking, 'OK, I did that. So what?' It's only now that I see what a big deal that was." Few Torchbearers take credit for their career success, even those who work in professions in which women are underrepresented. We met countless women who discount their own achievements even though they have won the admiration and respect of others who see them as trailblazers and their accomplishments as worthy of high praise.

Arlene, an educator and non-profit agency administrator, only recently recognized her innovative contributions to others as pioneering. "A Native American medicine man told this story and said it was about me: A father taught his young son how to plant corn. After the son grew up, his father said to him, 'You're really a good corn planter.' The young man replied, 'There's nothing to it.' His father asked him how he planted corn. The young man answered, 'You have to get the ground ready. Then you have to plant the seed just right. Finally, you have to do it at the right time of year when the rain and the sun are just right. But the sun, the seeds, and the rain are a part of nature and already there, so it's nothing special that I'm doing.' His father said to him, 'Yes, these things have always been there, but it took somebody to put them together.' So, for me, I look back at my work life and see that I created three very novel programs that now are established institutions in my community. Start-up stuff is hard. It takes a lot of work and energy. But I have come to realize that that is what I do. I'm a creator. I'm a corn planter."

New Truth: Be a seeker. Go beyond the beyond.

Some women view being a pioneer as a lifelong process that they continue to respect and honor in themselves. Janet doesn't see herself as someone who has broken new ground, but feels that she is a pioneer by virtue of her interest in raising consciousness. For her, pioneers are seekers who look for and explore new terrain. "The real liberation of women is in consciousness and spirit, rather than in what they've done in the material world," Janet says.

Cynthia sees herself as a pioneer because she's a risk-taker who feels free to move and make choices. What about breaking new ground? "I can't really say. That's for other people, for history, to determine. I found my own path. In my twenties, I broke new ground in my transition from drugs and a bad marriage to supporting myself financially and making a rich life for myself. Now in my forties, I'm in the ground-breaking mode again. I'm trying to find an integration point that allows me to participate in ways that are going to help heal the planet." The growing interest in spirituality suggests that this generation of women will have new territory, once again, in which to become pioneers.

"If you were to give advice to a younger generation of women, what would that advice be?"

> *"My daughter doesn't take a lot of advice. She is the most independent soul I've ever met. She does exactly what she wants to do, when she wants to do it. Several years ago, she and her boyfriend wanted to go to India. I was dead set against it and told her so. She said, 'Mom, I don't need your approval anymore, but I would like your blessing.' I looked at her and thought, 'Damn it! It took me twenty years to figure that out. How dare you recognize and understand yourself so quickly?' "*

Torchbearers have plenty of advice for younger women, but their most consistent message is to behave authentically in a way that comes from self-knowledge and self-respect. As a generation, they have keenly felt the absence of mentors in their own development. For this reason, they are eager to offer practical advice, based on their own experiences, so that other women may benefit.

When we asked what advice they have for younger women, they were ready to answer. Since this question was posed at the end of a lengthy interview, we initially attributed their short and rapid-fire replies to the fact that they were tired. This was not the case. After decades of trial and error and learning-by-doing, it appears that the women of this generation have been waiting a long time for someone to ask them to share their wisdom. While they addressed a variety of different themes, their two most recurrent messages to young women are "follow your dream" and "know thyself." Not very original ideas you might think, but remember, when they were young they *never* heard these messages. No one ever said, "Pursue your interests, have aspirations, trust your instincts." In fact, they were told quite the opposite.

Women who grew up in the 1950s were raised to believe they would get married, stay married, and live happily ever after. In the 1950s and 1960s, the main advice for middle-class females was "go to college, get married, and have kids—in that order." As young girls, they didn't know adult women who were divorced, or even worse, women who had never married at all. Even fewer knew career women who worked outside the home. At that time, there were few places where young women could go for guidance and direction in their lives.

Many women told us horrible stories about the career and college advice they received from high school guidance counselors who discouraged them from pursuing anything but the most traditional occupations. Even those with talent and a strong enthusiasm for certain fields of study, such as mathematics, were advised to not pursue their interests. The standard suggestion from a school counselor was, "If you like math so much, why don't you become a math teacher?" Mothers offered their own versions of career advice. As one woman said, "My mother always thought that being a secretary was a great job for me." In other words, "don't dream" and if you must dream, "dream small."

New Truth: Dream big and don't look at the glass ceiling.

"You can be anything." "Set high standards for yourself and don't accept mediocrity." "You go, girl!" We heard these ideas again and again. Because baby-boomer women never heard these messages themselves when they were young, there is both an urgency and a poignancy to the ferocity with which they urge young women to follow their dreams. One woman says, "Do whatever you want to do. This is not an issue that is open for discussion. It is your right. If someone tries to stop you, you should say, 'Excuse me, but I'm doing my life here!' " Many of the same words and phrases were used repeatedly: "Take risks." "Set goals." "Persevere." "Be somebody." "Accept no restrictions." "Set high standards for yourself." These are "power" messages meant to encourage young women and urge them on. As one business owner said, "Don't be afraid to be a personality, to be an individual, to stand out, to make something of yourself. These are important things to tell females because this is not an issue for men."

Along this line, there is agreement that meaningful work is essential in establishing a separate identity. Young women are repeatedly urged to find out what they want to do with their life and what will satisfy them. Connie, a business consultant, warns, "Don't do something just because somebody told you that you should do it. Do it because *you* want to." Sarah, an advertising executive, agrees, "I didn't know what I wanted to do when I graduated from college so I floundered for years and experimented with many different jobs. Now I tell young women to have a focus. 'What do you want to do with your life? What is going to satisfy you careerwise? What will enable you to become independent, to make your own living, to support yourself? Once you know what you want, take action.'" Sarah continues, "When I talk to women about how to get started, I tell them to get their credentials. If you don't have the educational background, get the experience. How do you do that if you don't have a job? Do volunteer work. It's an excellent way to get experience."

New Truth: Milk the enjoyment of your own awareness.

The second most frequently offered advice concerns trusting one's instincts and self-knowledge. "If your gut tells you something, it's probably true," Anita says. "As women, we have been trained to ignore our feelings and listen to others. Always follow your gut. Looking back at my life, I'm always surprised how incredibly on-the-spot my instincts were. When I didn't listen, I got into trouble every damn time." We heard a lot of admonitions about trusting guts, hearts, and bellies. Donna, a bank manager, offers this advice, "Always operate from the belly. Belly power—that's where the truth is. You know inside your body what's right, what's wrong, and what's true for you. Learn to trust that inner power and let it have a place in your life."

The women we interviewed are remarkably in agreement about how important it is not to censure oneself while acknowledging how difficult this is in the face of conservative forces that attempt to curtail choice and condemn assertive women. Diane, a software designer, warns, "Don't buy into what society says. We can spend years sorting those messages out before we ever get to our own personal stuff. Try to disregard all the hype about what we *should* be doing with our lives." She stresses how hard it is to remain true to yourself, "When I was younger, I never had a clear sense of who I was. I'm tart and stubborn and like to do things my own way, but I don't like the pain of my own mistakes. So put a toe in the water first and then follow your intuition." Another woman says, "Everybody has an inner voice that we don't always pay attention to. We waste too much of our lives living out the expectations of other people or society. All the answers are inside; some of us tune them out for whatever reason."

Finally, many urge young women to be more introspective about who they are separate from the men in their lives. This type of self-knowledge leads to greater self-comfort and increased self-pride. Andrea is a world traveler. When she was in college, she planned a three-month trip to Europe with one of her girlfriends. Her mother tried to talk her out of going. "She said, 'You shouldn't go to Europe. That's something you should wait and do when you're married.' Years later, whenever I was going to buy dishes or something for the kitchen, she would say, 'You should wait until you're married to buy that.' I told her I can go to Europe now and go again when I'm married. I can buy dishes now and get more later. I wasn't willing to sit around waiting for my life to begin."

12 incredibly smart pieces of advice for young women

1. Do not accept mediocrity.
2. You may be able to do it all, but you sure as hell can't do it all at once.

3. Develop the body you need to survive to eighty-plus years old. Don't be obsessed about conforming to some unattainable fantasy of beauty.
4. Your first career is not your only career.
5. Don't be intimidated by anyone.
6. Keep an eye on women's history so you have the stamina to continue your own generation's story.
7. Don't be afraid of failure, because there is no such thing.
8. Beware of anyone who claims to have the "solution."
9. Choice is not free.
10. Have somebody in your life, a mentor or role model, you can call on.
11. Don't be in a hurry or you'll miss out on the little things along the way.
12. Learn a skill you can carry with you anywhere.

"What do you anticipate your life will be like five years and thirty years from now?"

"I could be anywhere. I could get a promotion. I could be living in another place. I could be in another relationship. I don't know what my plans are. I don't have any five-year goals."

Torchbearers aren't planners. This is the flying-by-the-seat-of-your-pants, make-it-up-as-you-go-along generation. When asked about future plans, their answers were vague and imprecise. Many hope that there will be significant changes within the next five years with regard to relationships, children, and career. Spiritual development, financial security, health, and making a contribution to their community are also significant issues for the new millennium.

We asked the women we interviewed where they see themselves five and thirty years from now. Here is a sampling of what they said. Apart from those who don't anticipate major changes, a surprisingly large number answered: "I don't have a clue," "I have no goals," "I don't like that question," "I'm afraid to think about the future," "I have no idea," "I never plan my life," "It makes me nervous to think about it," "I hope I'm still alive," and "I have a hard time envisioning the future." We wonder how these women will make it into the 21st century! On closer examination, we found that despite these comments, many do indeed have hopes and dreams. In response to the question, "Where do you see yourself in five years?" their major projections involve career, the issue of children, spiritual/personal growth, relationship, and community involvement—in that order. We also discovered few have any concrete plans in place to make their aspirations a reality. The question "Where do you see yourself in thirty years?" generated even more abstract replies, with health, life enjoyment, making a contribution to others, and financial security mentioned most frequently.

By blazing unknown trails in their early adulthood, they learned quickly how to roll with the punches and go with the flow of life in order to survive. Without a doubt, the first generation to "be here now" has become quite skillful in finding their way without a map. Because they have had to focus on the present just to keep up, many adopted a somewhat cavalier attitude about the future. Because things have basically worked out so far, they assume that their future will also turn out well. While we hope that their adaptability, flexibility, and resourcefulness continue to serve them in good stead, we offer a caveat: the times they are a-changing once again. This generation will be living longer, and with fewer resources, than their parents. Perhaps a major shift in thinking needs to occur for the second half of life, one which will enable them to shape their futures more realistically and proactively.

New Truth: Live each day, but think realistically about the future.

Virginia, the unmarried forty-year-old owner of a small company, is noticing a definite change in herself as she looks toward the next five years. "I'm wondering if another door will open. Until now, everything has just happened. It's been unconscious. Now I'm reaching a point where I have to make sound decisions about what I will do with my life. Do I want to write a book? Do I want to be a mother, bake cookies, and be a Girl Scout leader? Knowing myself, whatever I do I'll give it my best shot." Several women mentioned starting a family as their goal. Joanne, a forty-one-year-old consultant, told us, "I hope I won't have to constantly worry about money. I want my business to be well established so I can have a child."

Virginia and Joanne will have to act quickly if they want to have children. And so will a surprising number of other forty-something women who still imagine not only getting pregnant, but also finding a husband first. Elizabeth, an unmarried forty-year-old with no immediate marriage prospects, says, "In the next five years, I hope to have one child. My business will pretty much be run by someone else. I'll be marketing and negotiating, doing what I do best. I'll be happily married without a doubt." Anita, a retailer, told us her plan, "One, get married and two, have kids." Ruth, a lawyer, says she is physically tired and has less energy due to her hectic schedule and the tremendous amount of stress she has at work. She never has time to relax, her mind is always running, and she is constantly thinking about all the things she has to do. What's her five-year plan? "I want to be in a good relationship with a man, and if he seemed like the right person, I'd like to have a child." None of these women said how they intend to pull this off. We couldn't help but wonder how realistic they are about their capacity to meet someone, marry, and have a child or two given that time on their biological clocks is running out.

In contrast, the forty-three-year-old owner of a distribution company voiced a dream consistent with her philosophy and financial resources. "I will adopt or have a child, even if there's no man in my life. I want to live in a big house in the country with a couple of kids, raising them to be the best they can be in a positive, nurturing environment. If I'm unable to have children, then I want to work with either the elderly or the homeless. I've worked all my life to be financially independent and now it's time to start frosting the cake, reaping the benefits, and contributing to society. The true source of happiness in life is how much you give back and help others."

Community involvement, giving back, and serving others are plans for the next five years for many women. One single mom is very clear about directing her energy toward the education of children. "I participate in the PTA and am actively involved in my son's education," she says. "I feel sorry for his teachers and the other parents because I'm opinionated. I'm an activist. I organize, march, and write letters. I do whatever it takes to find people who are of like mind and like thinking who want to be involved in public education, feel there's some hope, and believe they can make a difference. Our children's lives and emotional well-being are at stake. As American women, we must become the world's police because we recognize the problems in education and should take responsibility for fixing them."

Goals such as focusing on spiritual growth and personal development were mentioned by many women who spoke of their desire to live an easier and more joyful life, to work less, and relax more. "In five years, I'm going to be more at peace with myself. I hope my spiritual growth has a calming effect on me, because I'm fairly hyper. I want to get into 'being' instead of 'doing,'" said one woman. Another told us that she sees herself becoming an advocate, "My new voice is one that speaks out. I'm not afraid anymore to say what I know and I could care less what people think of me."

Relationship issues continue to surface. While most women intend to stay with their current partner, some express hope for changes in the relationship. A woman now dealing with relationship difficulties says, "In five years, my relationship will be more loving and less based on control, where we both can sit down and figure things out together. We can come to mutual understandings and develop workable solutions to whatever issues come up. I won't feel as if I have lost my identity. I'll be myself and my partner will love me for who I am." Others hope the relationship they are currently in does not change. "I see my relationship with this man going on until one of us kicks the bucket. Neither of us wants to get married or live together. We have his house, we have my house. Our lives are separate, but together." Finally, some hope for change, but don't expect it. "In the next five years I would like to find a relationship. I haven't found a man yet I can relate to, except on a superficial level, which is not enough for me. I'd rather be single than compromise."

New Truth: Act now as if you're going to live to be 100.

These women are singularly optimistic about how they want their lives to look in old age. "I hope I'm a wise old woman, very healthy and vibrant, and as interested in living my life as I am today. By then, my life experiences will have been interpreted to make me be a better and richer person inside," said one woman. Doreen, a human resources manager and a marathon runner, told us, "I'm going to be dynamite in thirty years. I will still be in great shape. When I first started training to run long distances, I saw this woman in her sixties jogging along a lot faster than me. I envision being like her." One liners were offered such as: "I want to be a tough old lady with lots of pep," "I'm going to be like a fine wine and improve with age," and, "I want to interact with young people and help them grow and develop with as much peace as possible."

Marcia, a hard-working entrepreneur, expects that her life will manifest a greater balance thirty years hence. "My life has been pretty much out of balance. I've never had that nice flow where there's time for relaxation, reading, and play because I'm always working. My priorities have been totally out of whack and I want that to change." A musician shared her image of aging, "I picture myself as being kind of scraggly and craggy with masses of long grey-white hair that I wear in a bun. I will still wear my hand-woven things and jeans and Nike shoes, have a great sense of humor, and lots of friends of all ages—in their teens, in their twenties, and in their eighties. I'll have published a book and will still play piano if the arthritis doesn't kill me."

Finally, one woman shared a vision for herself that has the potential to influence others as well. "In the future, women will have advanced into a realm of mega-consciousness. In thirty years, I expect to be hiking in Nepal, bouncing off the walls of a canyon, and just having a grand time being an elder and a wise old woman. I want a life that's solidly constructed and unified with nature. I want my bridges into other dimensions well-established by then. I want to be a servant of the people and to bring my vision to them."

The story continues…

> "Rocks need to be thrown in to start the waves moving out from the circle."

For the women of this generation to have the quality of life they want and so deserve in their later years, they will need to begin disturbing the still waters once again. To make their dreams and fantasies a reality, they must do what they did as young adults. Women must join together and break new ground once again. This time, their challenge will be to pioneer new ways for healthy women to age. They have worked hard and tolerated enormous amounts of stress throughout their adult lives. Although we encourage them to rest on their laurels a bit, create a better balance in their lives, and simply enjoy themselves more, we also urge them to "toss rocks into the water" now and then. They must initiate action today which will make the fulfillment of their future wants and needs possible, whether that is a house in the country, financial security, a loving relationship, the opportunity to help others, or inner peace.

Born into a time when assimilating new experiences into old structures no longer worked, the women of this generation were forced to construct new frameworks for thinking about themselves as adults. Along the way they gained resilience, inner strength, and an ability to problem solve in a wide variety of situations. As they move into their fifties, sixties, seventies, and beyond, they will continue to be agents of change. If they are unhappy with an aspect of their lives, they will surely make life-course modifications. We observed that no matter how successful or settled they appear to be, these women are actively engaged in the process of growth.

We encourage Torchbearers to accept that they deserve credit for their individual and generational achievements. They are members of a lucky generation, but it was not luck that brought them to where they are today. We urge them to internalize these messages: Thank your peers at every opportunity for standing by your side and offering support over the last thirty years. Continue reaching out, building on your successes, and testing out the waters. Remember that the only thing permanent is change. Be fearless. It's too late to care about what others may think of you because you've come too far and can never go back (thank God). Yours is a great legacy. You have left your footprints in the sand. Keep walking and remember to pass the torch.

A p p e n d i x

Interview Questions

Childhood through high school:

1. What was conventional and what was unconventional about your experiences growing up as a girl in the 1950s and the early 1960s?
2. What were your parents' aspirations for you?
3. What were your aspirations for yourself?
4. If you were an author, how would you title this chapter of your life?
5. Tell me two stories or anecdotes which capture your experiences during this period.

Young womanhood—college and the early twenties:

The 1960s were a time of political and social action. Some of the pivotal events or icons of this period include: the assassinations, the anti-war movement, the Chicago riots, the summer of love, the man on the moon, Kent State, VISTA/Peace Corps, the sexual revolution, the pill, hippies, Woodstock, drugs, gurus, communes, idealism, civil rights, SDS, the Black Panthers, the free speech movement, the counterculture, social causes, political activism, etc.—this list is suggestive, not exhaustive.

1. What was conventional and what was unconventional about your experiences as you moved from adolescence to young womanhood in the mid to late 1960s/early 1970s?
2. What were the major turning points in your life during those years and what were the effects of these?
3. If you were an author, how would you title this chapter of your life?
4. Tell me two stories or anecdotes which capture your experiences during this period.

The mid-twenties to mid-thirties:

The 1970s and early 1980s were a time of new roles, challenges, and opportunities for women. Some of the pivotal events or icons during this period include: the women's movement, consciousness raising groups, abortion (Roe v. Wade), wider occupational and professional possibilities, the search for self-expression, gay rights, divorce, discrimination, barriers, harassment, different types of sexual relationships, Watergate, being single, therapy, etc.—this list is suggestive, not exhaustive.

1. What was conventional and what was unconventional about your experiences as you moved from your mid- to late-twenties into your thirties in the 1970s and early 1980s?
2. What were the major turning points in your life during those years and what were the effects of these?
3. If you were an author, how would you title this chapter of your life?

4. Tell me two stories or anecdotes which capture your experiences during this period.

Mid-thirties to the present:

1. What has been conventional and what has been unconventional about your experiences as you moved from your mid- to late-thirties to your forties in the 1980s and 1990s?
2. What are the most central issues for you now and why: career, relationship, money, aging, health, fitness, parents, children, success, friendship, independence, goals, religion, spirituality, or...?
3. What have been the major turning points in your life during these years and what has been the effects of these?
4. If you were an author, how would you title this chapter of your life?
5. Tell me two stories or anecdotes which capture your experiences during this period.

Adult life self-reflections:

1. What is your parents' take on your life? What do they think explains why your life has turned out the way it has? What do you think explains why your life has turned out the way it has?
2. Have you had disillusioning experiences and, if so, what were the effects of these experiences e.g., empowering, sense of failure, self-blame, loss of trust, more realistic?
3. Would you describe yourself as a pioneer? How so?
4. Do you consider yourself a feminist? Why or why not?
5. What do you anticipate your life will be like in five years

(re: relationship, work, money, personal growth, spiritual development)? What do you anticipate your life will be like thirty years from now?

6. If you were to give advice to a younger generation of women, what would that advice be?

Please respond to the following:

1. Our generation had no rules—it was not possible to follow the path of a previous generation. We had a wider variety of choices and if we didn't like those, we could invent new choices. How has this affected the women of our generation?
2. The women of our generation changed more than the men of our generation (this was true in the 1970s and it is still true today). Many men seem egalitarian on the surface but they remain traditional underneath. Has this been your experience in your romantic relationships with men?
3. Women of our generation have different kinds of connections and interdependencies and commitments from previous generations. Who is your family now?
4. Unlike women in their twenties and early thirties, women of our generation carry the baggage of the pre-liberation era. In other words, there are two competing models for women our age: the traditional model of the 1950s and the feminist model of the 1970s. In what ways do these models manifest themselves in your life?

Is there anything you would like to add or any questions you would like to ask?

1999 © Susan B. Evans, Ed.D., and Joan P. Avis, Ph.D.

Resources and References

Anderson, S. & Hopkins, P. (1991). *The feminine face of God: The unfolding of the sacred in women*. New York: Bantam Books.

Bateson, C. (1990). *Composing a life*. New York: Plume.

Bridges, W. (1980). *Transitions: Making sense of life's changes*. New York: Perseus Press.

Brown, H. G. (1982) *Having it all*. New York: Simon & Schuster.

Campbell, B. M. (1993). *Successful women, angry men: Backlash in the two-career marriage*. New York: Random House.

Conway, J. K. (1998). *When memory speaks*. New York: Vintage Books.

Davidson, S. (1997). *Loose change: Three women of the '60s*. Berkeley: University of California Press.

Edwards, A. & Polite, C. (1992). *Children of the dream*. New York: Doubleday.

Ehrenreich, B. (1991). *The worst years of our lives*. New York: Harper Collins.

Ehrenreich, B., Hess, E., & Jacobs, G. (1986). *Remaking love: The feminization of sex*. New York: Anchor Books.

Eichenbaum, L. & Orbach, S. (1988). *Between women*. New York: Viking.

Goldberg, N. (1998). *Writing down the bones: Freeing the writer within*. Boston: Shambala Press.

Gilligan, C. (1982). *In a different voice: Psychological theory and women's development*. Cambridge, MA: Harvard University Press.

Faludi, S. (1991). *Backlash: The undeclared war against American women*. New York: Crown.

Fleming, A. T. (1995). *Motherhood deferred: A woman's journey*. New York: Fawcett.

French, M. (1986). *Beyond power: On women, men and morals*. New York: Ballantine.

Hancock, E. (1990). *The girl within*. New York: Fawcett.

Heimel, C. (1992). *If you can't live without me, why aren't you dead yet?* New York: Harper Perennial.

Hewlett, S. (1986). *A lesser life*. New York: Warner Books.

Josselson, R. (1987). *Finding herself: Pathways to identity development in women*. New York: Jossey-Bass.

Kaminer. W. (1994). *I'm dysfunctional, you're dysfunctional: The recovery movement and other self-help fashions*. New York: Vintage.

Levinson, D. (1986). *Season's of a man's life*. New York: Ballantine.

Mead, M. (1995). *Blackberry winter: My early years*. New York: Kodansha.

McMillan, T. (1994). *Waiting to exhale*. New York: Washington Square.

Merser, C. (1987). *Grown-ups*. New York: Plume.

Moorman, J. (1986). *The history and the future of the relationship between education and marriage*. U.S. Bureau of the Census.

Munsch, R. (1988). *The paperbag princess*. New York: Annick Press.

Quindlen, A. (1993). *Thinking out loud*. New York: Random House.

Quindlen, A. (1994). *Living out loud*. New York: Fawcett.

Ryff, C. & Keyes, C. L. (1995). *The structure of psychological well-being revisited*. Journal of Personality and Social Psychology, 69 (4), 719–727.

Rix, S. (Ed.) (1990). *The American woman*. New York: Beacon.

Sheehy, G. (1996). *New Passages: Mapping your life across time*. New York: Ballantine.

Sheehy, G. (1984). *Passages*. New York: Bantam.

Smith, C. (1988). *Why women shouldn't marry*. Secaucus, NJ: Lyle Press.

Tomlin, L. (1991). *The search for signs of intelligent life in the universe*. New York: Harper Collins.

Wasserstein, W. (1998). *American daughter*. New York: Harcourt Brace.

Wasserstein, W. (1991). *Bachelor girls*. New York: Vintage.

PHOTO: LARRY DYER

About the Authors

Susan B. Evans, Ed.D., and Joan P. Avis, Ph.D., are professors at the University of San Francisco. Susan teaches graduate courses in special education, survey research, and data analysis. Joan is a licensed psychologist who specializes in adult development and life planning and is the Director of the Life Transitions Institute in San Francisco. They are both members of the generation of women who broke all the rules.

Stories to Tell?

Many stories of the Torchbearer generation have yet to be told. If you have an extraordinary story to share about your experience as a member of this generation, please send it to the following address, along with your name, address, and telephone number:

Life Transitions Institute
450 Sutter St. Suite 2103
San Francisco, CA 94108-4206

You will be contacted if the material will be considered for subsequent publication.

Dr. Evans and Dr. Avis offer *The Women Who Broke All the Rules* Seminars. They also are available as speakers and consultants in the areas of women's issues, balancing love and work, motivation and empowerment, adult development and life planning, leadership, collaboration, and creating life quality for women of all ages.

You may contact Susan and Joan through their website at www.womenwhobroketherules.com, by e-mail (evanss@usfca.edu; avisj@usfca.edu), or by telephone (415-956-9516).